The Vegetarian
NO-CHOLESTEROL
Barbecue
Cookbook

The
Vegetarian
NO-CHOLESTEROL
Barbecue
Cookbook

by Kate Schumann and
Virginia Messina, M.P.H., R.D.

St. Martin's Press • New York

The recipe for Nasturtiums Filled with Guacamole is from Flowers in the Kitchen. *The author, Susan Belsinger, and the publisher, Interweave Press, generously allowed us to reprint it.*
The salad dressing in Mystery Garden Oriental Salad appeared in The Pasta Salad Book *by Nina Graybill and Maxine Rapoport. Permission to include it was given by the publisher, Farragut Publishing Company.*

Design by Liney Li

Library of Congress Cataloging-in-Publication Data

Schumann, Kate.
    The vegetarian no-cholesterol barbecue cookbook / Kate Schumann and Virginia Messina.
       p.   cm.
    ISBN 0-312-11106-1
    1. Vegetarian cookery.   2. Barbecue cookery.   I. Messina, Virginia.   II. Title.
RM236.S37   1994
641.5'636—dc20   94-2006
                                                               CIP

First Edition: May 1994

10 9 8 7 6 5 4 3 2 1

With much love and thanks to our husbands,
Ned Schumann and Mark Messina,
who enthusiastically taste-tested recipe after recipe,
and who never once complained,
"We're having veggie burgers for dinner *again*!?"

Contents

Acknowledgments

First and foremost, we thank all the people who so generously provided us with their favorite vegetarian burgers. They were the inspiration for this book and we appreciate the wonderful recipe ideas they shared.

We're grateful to the staff at the Physicians Committee for Responsible Medicine for their support with this project. Special thanks go to Carter Ross and Chrissie Bartlett for their assistance and to Neal Barnard for helping to get the project off the ground.

Gail Naftalin and Theresa Boardwine generously provided their culinary expertise in helping us select the "world's best veggie burgers."

We owe heartfelt thanks to our energetic agent Patti Breitman for her advice and for her never-waning enthusiasm for this book. To the staff at St. Martin's Press, especially Jennifer Weis and Todd Keithley, goes our appreciation for their patience and expertise—and for putting up with a couple of free-spirited cooks.

Introduction

Who would have thought that the quest to find the perfect vegetarian burger would give birth to a whole book on barbecuing? But that's exactly what happened. We invited would-be chefs across the country to send us their favorite recipes for a burger that could be cooked on the grill; the response was nothing short of extraordinary. It seemed that everyone had a wonderful burger to share. And those who didn't have a veggie burger recipe wanted to find one, judging from the number of requests we had for the winning recipe.

Grilling and barbecuing are favorite ways to cook in the summer. After all, what other activity combines the casualness and ease of grilling with that feeling of luxury that accompanies dining al fresco? And talk about great taste! Nothing beats food cooked over the coals or over smoky, aromatic mesquite. But while everybody loves to grill, people also want alternatives to the usual fatty fare. Also, the National Cancer Institute warns that charcoal-broiled meats produce carcinogens, and raise your risk of getting cancer.

This book is a new approach to summer food. The recipes build on common barbecue menus—but with a creative twist that is both fun and healthful. We think that you will agree that barbecuing has never tasted so great, or been so enjoyable. Imagine thick, juicy vegetable "steaks," brushed with a lemon marinade, then nicely charred on a grill and stuffed into crusty French rolls. Or, if an old-fashioned burger on a bun is more your style, how about Cajun Grills, P-Nutty Garden Burgers with Sunny Relish, or Bangkok Bean Burgers with Peanut Cilantro Sauce. Then round out your picnic fare with salads like Pasta Apricot Salad or New Zealand Brown Rice with Kiwi. Top it all off with a cooling watermelon sorbet, or some fresh fruit grilled to juicy perfection.

You will also find plans and menus that will turn any occasion into a picnic, from the raucous birthday party of a six-year-old to the most elegant of garden parties. There are menus with an international flair, such as our Mexican Fiesta Picnic, and those that are decidedly patriotic like the Old-Fashioned Fourth of July Family Cookout.

These recipes were designed for people who love good food and who want to eat healthfully. In the pages that follow you will find an eating experience that fits right in with the joyful ease of warm summer evenings and lighthearted summer days.

CHAPTER ONE

Tips
for Grilling

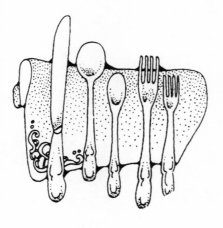

Whether your preference is for the backyard barbecue, a portable picnic in the park, or food cooked over a glowing fire at a remote campsite, the essence of grilling is simplicity. Grilling imparts such lovely flavors to foods—and the whole outdoor cooking experience is such fun—that it is easy to put together a memorable meal using basic foods and simple recipes.

If you are having a crowd over for a holiday picnic, toss together a burger mix the night before and refrigerate. Then serve it with a salad, some baked beans, and several sides of grilled vegetables, brushed with olive oil and herbs.

If you are planning a quick supper for the family, don't get too elaborate with main courses and side dishes. Grilled eggplant on French bread served with a green salad and potatoes that have been baked in the coals is a wonderful, satisfying, and healthy meal that requires almost no preparation time.

Grilling is perfect for weekday cooking, when you might feel too tired to put a big dinner together. When you get home from work, cut up three or four different vegetables and some chunks of tofu and drizzle a fast marinade over them. Then light the charcoal and let it heat up while the veggies marinate and you relax. By the time you've changed your clothes, fed the dog, and opened the mail, the food is ready to toss on the grill. With a loaf of good bread you have one of the summer's best dinners with no fuss and virtually no time spent cooking.

Your cooking gear should be simple, too. You don't need any fancy tools, but might want to consider a few of the following:

Skewers: Choose skewers that are flat on two sides to keep food from spinning around. Or run two parallel skewers through the food to hold it in place. Wooden skewers look pretty, but metal ones cook the food faster.

Basting Brush: The long-handled kind designed especially for barbecuing is especially nice since it allows you to keep your hands away from the heat of the fire, but any kind of basting brush will do.

Metal Spatula: This is essential, of course, for turning burgers and vegetable "steaks." Again, the long-handled kind is nice, but not absolutely necessary.

Chimney Charcoal Starter: Many grilling enthusiasts, ourselves included, swear by this. It is a foolproof method for starting coals without soaking them first with starter fluid. It looks like a giant's tin cup with a wooden handle. Just crumple two sheets of newspaper in the bottom, put in as many briquettes as you need, light a match to the paper, and in about 12 to 15 minutes you have wonderfully hot coals. Dump them out on your grill and you are ready to go.

You can also make your own simple version from a large coffee can. Remove the bottom with a can opener and punch holes around the can a few inches above the bottom. Then set the can on top of the coal grate and crumble some paper in the bottom. Pour in the coals and light the paper. Once the coals are burning well, lift the can out of the grill (with a pair of tongs) and spread the coals in the bottom.

Electric Starters: If you have an outlet near your grill you can use one of these metal coils to get the coals going. Just plug it in and put the metal end in the mound of charcoal. It will light in just a few minutes.

Lighter Fluid: We shy away from this simply because it is so flammable. If it gets on your hands or clothing, it can be dangerous. It's also toxic if some of it gets on the food. Since both methods for starting coals noted above are so simple, there is really no reason to use lighter fluid.

Grilling Baskets versus Grilling Screens: Grilling baskets allow you to sandwich your burger between two long-handled metal grids which close snugly over the burgers. Since a basket will hold four to six burgers, you can flip them all at once, or lift them easily away from the fire if it gets too hot. These are great tools for campfire cooks, too, since they allow you to cook food over an open fire when a grill isn't available.

Grilling screens are a more popular choice for home grillers. These fine-meshed screens are designed for cooking delicate foods like vegetables that might otherwise slip through the cooking grill. We consider them to be absolutely essential for our grilling recipes, which tend to produce more delicate foods.

· TYPES OF GRILLS ·

COVERED VERSUS OPEN GRILLS

Open grills represent the oldest form of cooking—a grate over a fire. Some, like hibachis, are small and portable and can go along on picnics or camping trips with you. Uncovered grills usually have adjustable cooking surfaces so that you can control how far away food is from the fire.

The traditional kettle grill, such as the kind made by Weber, is the most common of the covered grills. Covers are valuable for foods that need to cook for a long time; since vegetables and meatless burgers tend to cook quickly, there is less reason to use a cover. Also, most covered grills don't have grates that you can raise or lower. One advantage to covered grills, however, is that fire flare-ups are generally avoided and food is less likely to be burned.

Grills usually burn either charcoal or wood, or they use gas. Gas grills are preferred by some because they are less messy and are easy to start. However, unless you use some type of aromatic ingredient like mesquite chips, food cooked on a gas grill tastes like food cooked in the kitchen. Gas grills use natural gas or propane gas for fuel to heat reusable lava rock. The heat from the rock cooks the food. Advantages are that there are no ashes to dispose of and the grills are easier to clean. They also heat up much faster—in about 5 minutes; charcoal grills take at least 20 minutes to produce enough heat for cooking and can take as long as 30 minutes to get really hot.

☐ *Types of Charcoal*

If you are cooking over coal, there are two kinds to choose from: charcoal briquettes or lump charcoal. Briquettes are made from ground charcoal and binders to hold it together. They often have additives that make them easy to light. They're the most commonly used charcoal and they impart that familiar charcoal smell.

Lump charcoal is made from hardwood such as apple, maple, oak, or mesquite and it imparts the flavor of the wood to food. Some people prefer it because it contains no additives. While lump charcoal is more expensive than briquettes, it gets hotter and stays hot longer than briquettes, so you get your money's worth. Lump charcoal can cause the cooking grill to heat up to more than 600 degrees while briquettes produce a temperature of about 350 degrees.

You'll find that cooking time varies a lot, depending on the type of charcoal you use. For all of our recipes, we've used charcoal briquettes. But don't be afraid to try lump charcoal, bearing in mind that food will cook slightly faster.

Cooking with Wood: Larger grills, and campfires, can burn wood as well as charcoal. Food cooked over wood can have a lovely flavor, depending on the kind of wood used. For even burning, and the best cooked food, try maple, hickory, oak, dogwood, beech, birch, or ash.

Aromatics: Give your fire some extra pizzazz by tossing in wood chips or shredded wood with wonderful aromas. Mesquite, hickory, and apple are among the most popular. Soak them first in a little water and then toss a handful into the fire. (Don't overdo it or your fire may fizzle.) You can also use fresh or dried herbs to create a nice aroma that will subtly permeate the food. Sprinkle a handful of fresh rosemary, thyme, bay, oregano, mint, or other favorite herbs into the fire. Try juniper berries for a subtle pinelike scent.

COOKING ON THE GRILL

Cooking on a grill is quite a different prospect from cooking on a stove, where the temperature is easily adjusted and regulated. Expect to experiment a little when you try a new food on the grill. The final product will be affected by how hot the fire is and how far from the fire the cooking grill is.

Part of the secret lies in knowing when your fire is ready. With a gas grill, it is pretty easy. The grill is ready about 5 minutes after you light it. With coals you need to wait until a light ash forms on the outside of the coals.

Arrange the coals in a mound in the center of your grill, tapering off a bit in depth as the mound approaches the sides of the grill. It's a good idea to leave a section around the perimeter of the grill with no coals. That way, you will have a very hot center for cooking, but the heat will taper off toward the outside of the grill and you'll have a spot where you can move foods to keep them warm without having them cook further.

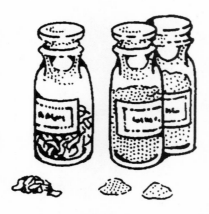

CHAPTER TWO

A Healthy Menu

Something happens to unhealthy eating habits when they get moved outdoors: They get even worse.

For most people, a backyard barbecue means thick greasy steaks or burgers, fatty chicken pieces, and mounds of mayonnaise-drenched salads. These holiday picnics mirror our everyday eating habits, only they include just a little bit more of everything we do wrong.

Most Americans eat too much fat and protein and too many calories. We pay the price for these excesses with some of the world's highest rates of heart disease, obesity, colon and breast cancer, and diabetes.

Fortunately, it's easy to make the shift towards a healthier eating style. And the habits of a healthy diet work just as well outdoors as in the kitchen.

Healthy eating can be summed up in one sentence. It is a diet based on whole plant foods: grains, vegetables, beans, and fruits. The effects of revising your menus to feature more of these foods are dramatic.

Menus based on plant foods are lower in cholesterol, and those that use* only *plant foods are cholesterol-free. Cholesterol is found only in animal products. You may have thought that "no-cholesterol" means choosing leaner cuts of meat, but that won't do the trick. Cholesterol is actually found in the lean portion of animal tissues. So a piece of chicken *without* the skin has just as much cholesterol as a piece of chicken *with* the skin. Lean ground beef and ground turkey have the same amount of cholesterol as regular ground beef.

In contrast, plant foods never contain any cholesterol. Even higher-fat plant foods like avocados, coconuts, and nuts are cholesterol-free.

Plant foods also tend to be lower in total fat and are much lower in saturated fat than animal products. Saturated fat pushes blood cholesterol levels up more than any other food component.

Menus based on plant foods contain ample protein, but are not excessive in this nutrient. The kind and amount of protein you eat can also affect your blood cholesterol levels. Replacing the animal protein in your diet with plant protein, such as the protein found in beans and grains, helps to reduce blood cholesterol levels dramatically. This is completely independent of the amount of fat in the diet. This may be one reason why vegetarians have much lower levels of blood cholesterol and less heart disease.

Protein from animal products also causes excess calcium to be lost from the body and might contribute to weakened bones.

If you are worried that a barbecue of vegetables will shortchange your guests on protein, don't be. The average American eats about twice the protein recommended. People who eat only vegetables and other plant foods have a protein intake that is much closer to the recommended dietary allowances. In the case of protein, less is better than more, and plant protein is better than animal protein.

Menus based on plant foods are rich in fiber. Fiber is found only in plant foods. Diets based on meat and dairy products are bound to be too low in fiber. Low-fiber diets are associated with a greater risk of colon disease, including colon cancer. Fiber also helps to reduce cholesterol, and for diabetics, can help to regulate blood glucose levels.

Plant foods provide naturally occurring chemicals that fight cancer and heart disease. Plant foods are loaded with chemicals—called phytochemicals—with anticancer properties. Many of these also reduce the risk for heart disease. These phytochemicals operate in a variety of ways, but some of them seem to have powerful positive effects.

Meat on the grill: double trouble. Meat-based diets are associated with health problems because they are high in cholesterol, fat, and animal protein, and are low in fiber. But there is a double risk when you cook that meat on a grill. Grilling meat, chicken, or fish causes animal fat to drip into the coals. The resultant smoke that rises from the coals and coats the meat contains benzopyrene, a cancer-causing substance related to the tar in cigarette smoke.

Other compounds, called heterocyclic aromatic amines or HAAs, are formed from the breakdown of protein in meats when they are cooked at especially high temperatures, as in grilling.

The risk of consuming these foods may be considerable. Leading cancer authorities, including the National Cancer Institute, warn consumers about the dangers of consuming charcoal-broiled meats.

• UNINVITED GUESTS •

There is one more health advantage to no-cholesterol cookouts. Foods high in protein, like meats, poultry, and fish, are especially prone to bacterial contamination. A bout with salmonella poisoning will cause any happy picnic memories to fade in a flash. But burgers made of whole grains and beans are much less likely to carry salmonella and other bacteria. Also, they are less likely to spoil, and it isn't necessary to cook them to a crisp to kill any bacteria. Most of our burgers can be cooked fast, until they are golden on the outside and heated through, but still moist and fresh. Do bear in mind, however, that no matter what kind of food you are eating, food poisoning is always a potential problem. If food will sit for a while before or after you cook, be sure to keep it in a cooler.

• PLANNING HEALTHY MENUS •

We said earlier that it is easy to define a healthy way of eating: Just eat more whole grains, vegetables, beans, and fruits. A nice surprise is that it is so easy to come up with an endless variety of exceptional meals using these foods. Along the way you will become acquainted with delightful foods that are a part of many international cuisines. Most are easy to prepare and will add exquisite new flavors to your menus.

The first step toward healthy eating is to base your meals on hearty whole grains. These include familiar fare like whole grain breads, rice, and cereals. But this group of foods also includes some less familiar grains like couscous, quinoa, amaranth, bulgur, wheat berries, and millet. It is easy to find ways to include these foods in every meal. Enjoy whole grain breads or muffins with hot cereal for breakfast. Lunches can be familiar favorites like sandwiches on whole grain bread or pasta salad with vegetables. Fill your dinner plate with a fluffy mound of rice, quinoa, or couscous topped with steamed vegetables.

To boost your intake of fruits and vegetables, snack on these foods throughout the day and include them in as many meals as you can. Visit the produce section of your grocery store with a fresh perspective; there are probably many items there that you have never tried before, including wonderful tropical fruits and all kinds of interesting Asian vegetables.

Include a serving or two of legumes in your daily menu. Legumes are beans, peas, and lentils. Some, like refried beans, lentil soup, or baked beans, may already be a part of your diet. There are literally hundreds of different kinds of beans consumed throughout the world. You'll find a good variety in your local grocery store and will discover many more in international food markets. A good way to add legumes to your diet is to enjoy soyfoods such as tofu or tempeh. These are great meat-replacers both on the grill and indoors.

Not all plant foods are low in fat. Nuts and seeds, peanut butter, avocados, and vegetable oils are high-fat items. Like all plant foods, they are free of cholesterol, however, and (excepting vegetable oils) they are loaded with fiber and with the chemicals that fight cancer. Use these foods in moderation in your diet. We've included nuts in some of our burgers for the special crunch and flavor they add. Even with the addition of moderate amounts of these ingredients, our burgers are still lower in fat than standard grilled fare.

Our recipes for no-cholesterol cookouts will introduce you to some plant foods that you may never have tried before. Once you have tried them on the grill, in a salad, or as part of a burger recipe, you'll feel confident about including these foods in some of your regular cooking. When you discover how enjoyable no-cholesterol cookouts are, you will probably want to try this new style of eating indoors.

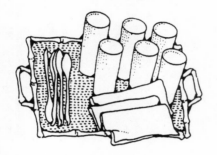

CHAPTER THREE

On the Grill: Burgers and Other Grillables

Anything goes on the grill, but foods that withstand fast, hot cooking do best. That's why vegetables and burgers made from grains and vegetables are perfect choices.

In fact, our burgers may just change the way you think about picnics and barbecues. Although toppings are a part of the burger ritual, you'll find that these burgers are so flavorful—and that their flavors are so wonderfully unique—that you may not want to drown them in catsup and mustard. In fact, our tasters commented that they preferred many of the burgers by themselves, without the trappings of pickles and condiments, or even a bun. They wanted to enjoy the special flavors of the burger rather than losing them in bread and toppings.

You can enjoy the burgers any way you like. A number of them include a recipe for a special topping or sauce that enhances the taste of the burger. Tuck them into a light pita pocket instead of a burger roll, or serve them up on a slice of crusty French bread.

Since our burgers contain no meat, you can taste the burger mix before you grill and adjust the seasonings. Most of the mixtures keep well. Shape them into patties, place squares of waxed paper between them, wrap well, and freeze for later use.

These burgers are much lower in fat than traditional beef and even than patties made from ground turkey. They are also lower in the proteins that coagulate during cooking and bind the ingredients together. For these reasons, our more delicate versions don't hold together quite as tenaciously as meat burgers. Grilling screens or baskets designed for cooking low-fat foods on the grill are perfect for these burgers.

If you don't have the time or the inclination to make a burger mix, plain vegetables on the grill are a simple and appealing alternative. They are absolutely delectable and easy to prepare. Soak them in one of our marinades first for several hours if you like, or just brush them lightly with oil and then dust with herbs before grilling. Because vegetables are virtually fat-free, they tend to stick to the grill, making them difficult to flip. For that reason, if the vegetables haven't been marinated in a sauce that contains a little oil, we recommend brushing them on both sides with just a touch of olive oil before grilling. Bear in mind that we are talking about a very light brush of oil. A thick eggplant "steak" might have just ½ teaspoon of oil brushed on it, giving it a total of 2½ grams of fat. Compare that to a hamburger made from extra lean ground beef, which has 16 grams of fat, or a piece of barbecued chicken with 13 grams of fat.

The following recipes will make your mouth water and will take your barbecuing experience into an entirely new realm of cooking. Read on, and enjoy.

The Vegetarian No-Cholesterol Barbecue Cookbook

Chinese-style Black Bean Burgers

• •

This delicious burger was sent to us by Sarah Flanders, a medical student and a strong advocate of preventive medicine. We added a bit of Chinese curry powder (it does not contain cumin as does Indian curry powder) and five-spice powder, an exotic-tasting blend of star anise, ginger, cinnamon, fennel seed, and black pepper.

1 cup canned black beans
10 ounces firm tofu, drained and patted dry
1⅓ cups thinly sliced cabbage
1 tablespoon canola oil
½ cup finely chopped onion
½-inch piece fresh ginger, minced
1 clove garlic, peeled and finely chopped
½ cup fine dry bread crumbs
1½ tablespoons miso or 2 tablespoons soy sauce
¼ to ½ teaspoon Chinese curry powder
¼ to ½ teaspoon five-spice powder

Mash beans in a bowl with tofu.

Steam shredded cabbage just until bright green and beginning to soften.

In 1 tablespoon canola oil, sauté onion, ginger, and garlic until onion is soft.

Combine all the prepared ingredients with bread crumbs, miso or soy sauce, curry powder, and five-spice powder. Add more bread crumbs if necessary until mixture has a consistency suitable for forming into patties.

Make 6 patties, place in a grilling basket, and grill until both sides are lightly browned.

★ SERVES 6

ℬasic ℬean ℬurgers

Victoria Schiloni, who owns and operates a vegetarian catering service in Philadelphia, created this burger. It uses TVP (texturized vegetable protein), a soy product available in natural foods stores.

1 scant cup boiling water
1 cup TVP granules
1 tablespoon tomato paste or catsup
One 16-ounce can pinto, kidney, or other beans, drained
¼ cup fresh whole wheat bread crumb cubes
2 cloves garlic, peeled and finely minced
½ teaspoon oregano
1 tablespoon tamari or soy sauce
1 teaspoon sugar
Salt and pepper to taste
Whole wheat flour for dusting

Pour boiling water over TVP and tomato paste in a bowl. Stir and let rest for 10 minutes.

In food processor, combine TVP mixture with remaining ingredients except for flour. Pulse until mixture is almost a purée.

Dust hands with flour and shape mixture into 6 burgers. Dust them lightly in flour. Layer the burgers between sheets of waxed paper and refrigerate for at least 1 hour.

Cook on a grill covered with foil for about 10 minutes on each side.

★ SERVES 6

Peanut Burgers with Satay Sauce

· ·

This is Victoria Schiloni's peanut-y variation on her Basic Bean Burger.

Follow the directions for Basic Bean Burgers with the following changes: Omit the oregano and add 1 teaspoon fresh minced ginger. During the last pulse of the food processor add ¼ cup chopped peanuts, leaving them crunchy. Form mixture into 6 patties as described above and serve with satay sauce.

❧ SATAY SAUCE

1 small onion, peeled and minced
1 clove garlic, peeled and minced
1 small chile pepper, seeded and chopped
1 teaspoon sesame oil
1 teaspoon corn oil
1 cup natural chunky peanut butter
¼ cup teriyaki sauce
2 teaspoons brown sugar
¼ cup water
1 tablespoon tomato paste
1 tablespoon sesame tahini*
Salt and pepper to taste

In a heavy saucepan sauté the onion, garlic, and chile pepper in the sesame oil and corn oil. When translucent, add the peanut butter and stir until melted. Add the rest of the ingredients. Simmer over medium heat for 10 minutes. Serve over grilled peanut burgers.

*Tahini is sesame butter. It can be found in the international food section of your grocery store, in most health food stores, and in Middle Eastern markets.

★ SERVES 6

Bangkok Bean Burgers with Peanut Cilantro Sauce

. . . .

Carol Ann Islam of Corvallis, Oregon, created this burger with a touch of Thailand.

1 pound firm tofu
1 cup cooked black beans, well drained
¾ cup raw quick-cooking oats
½ cup red onion, peeled and finely chopped
½ cup carrots, peeled and finely grated
1 tablespoon plus 1 teaspoon grated fresh ginger root
1 tablespoon tamari or soy sauce
2 tablespoons packed brown sugar
2 large cloves garlic, peeled and minced
1 to 1½ teaspoons red pepper flakes
Vegetable oil
Flour for dusting
Thin slices peeled cucumber

Squeeze tofu in paper towels to discard excess water, then mash it in a large bowl. Add rest of ingredients except for oil, flour, and cucumbers. Mix well.

Form mixture into 8 patties. Lightly brush both sides of patties with vegetable oil and dust with flour.

Brush grill rack with oil. Cook over medium hot coals about 4 minutes on each side. Serve on toasted buns and top with peanut cilantro sauce and cucumber slices.

★ SERVES 8

❦ PEANUT CILANTRO SAUCE

3 tablespoons natural crunchy peanut butter
3 tablespoons fresh lemon juice
¼ cup minced fresh cilantro

In a small bowl, blend peanut butter and lemon juice. Mix in cilantro to combine.

Grilled Eggplant Steaks

• •

Eggplant is one of our favorite vegetables for the grill. Cooked until just slightly charred, and served in a crusty roll, it tastes like a rare delicacy.

2 large eggplants
Salt
¼ cup olive oil
Juice of 1 lemon
1 teaspoon thyme
⅛ teaspoon black pepper

Slice the eggplant into ½-inch slices. Sprinkle with salt, layer in a colander, and allow to sit for 1 hour.

In a bowl combine the olive oil, lemon juice, thyme, and pepper and mix thoroughly.

Rinse the eggplant slices and pat dry with a paper towel. Brush each slice with the lemon mixture. Grill on each side until just lightly browned. Serve on crusty rolls with lettuce and slices of tomato.

★ SERVES 8

Mushroom Barley Burgers

· ·

These burgers get rave reviews at the Berwyn Cafe in College Park, Maryland, where they were created by cook Ji-Hyon Kim. With their pleasant texture and delicate herby flavor, they will be a hit at your backyard barbecues, too.

> 1½ cups uncooked barley
> 3 cups water
> 1½ cups water
> 1 cup rolled oats
> 2 medium cloves garlic, peeled and pressed
> 1 teaspoon garlic powder
> 1 medium onion, peeled and finely chopped
> 1 large stalk celery, minced
> 1 teaspoon each marjoram and basil, OR 1 teaspoon
>   Italian seasoning, OR 1 tablespoon fresh snipped dill
> 2 teaspoons olive oil
> 1 pound mushrooms, coarsely chopped
> ¼ cup sesame tahini
> ¼ cup sunflower seeds
> 1½ tablespoons low-sodium soy sauce

Cook barley in 3 cups water and set aside.

Boil 1½ cups water, then add oats. Leave covered, turn off heat, and set aside.

In a frying pan, sauté garlic cloves, garlic powder, onion, celery, and herbs in 2 teaspoons olive oil until onion is slightly translucent. Add chopped mushrooms and continue cooking until most of the liquid has evaporated.

Combine all ingredients in a bowl and mix until evenly blended. Form eight 3-inch burgers and grill until brown on each side.

★ SERVES 8

Beet this Burger

. . . .

This burger comes from Olinda Cho-Forsythe, a native of Guatemala and a full-blooded Mayan. She developed her burger recipe in the kitchens of the Gran Fraternidad Universal, an organization dedicated to world peace and to promoting a vegetarian diet through its centers and restaurants throughout Latin America. The unusual addition of 1 tablespoon of grated beets is just enough to give this burger a pleasant color.

1 tablespoon finely grated raw beet

½ cup cooked oats

1 cup uncooked oats

½ cup coarsely ground walnuts

¼ cup coarsely ground almonds

2 tablespoons sesame seeds

1 tablespoon nutritional yeast flakes (optional)

¼ cup minced green pepper

¼ cup minced onion

1 teaspoon dried basil

¼ teaspoon dried thyme

¼ teaspoon ground sage

¼ teaspoon mustard powder

2 tablespoons soy sauce

1 tablespoon instant dry vegetable broth

Tomato slices, for garnish

Mix all ingredients together well. Form into 6 patties and grill until cooked through. Serve on whole wheat rolls with tomato slices and your favorite condiments.

★ SERVES 6

Ratatouille Burgers

· · · · · · · · · · · · · · · · · · · ·

Wonderful flavors of the herbs and vegetables of the Mediterranean make this burger a summer favorite. We found these burgers to be very delicate and so, for outdoor grilling, we suggest you add the vegetarian refried beans to help them hold together better.

3 tablespoons peanut oil

1 small eggplant, unpeeled, coarsely chopped (about 3 cups)

1 cup chopped unpeeled zucchini

1 cup coarsely chopped fresh mushrooms

1 small onion, peeled and chopped

2 garlic cloves, peeled and minced

1 sweet red pepper, seeded and chopped

½ sweet green or yellow pepper, seeded and chopped

8 ounces tofu, drained and mashed

⅓ cup minced parsley leaves

1 teaspoon dried oregano

⅛ teaspoon cumin

Salt and pepper to taste

1 teaspoon dried basil

½ tablespoon maple syrup (optional)

⅔ cups toasted wheat germ

½ cup crumb stuffing mix

1 medium tomato, seeded and chopped

½ to ⅔ cup canned vegetarian refried beans (optional), OR
*   2 to 3 tablespoons whole wheat flour*

8 sesame buns

In a large skillet, heat oil. Add eggplant, zucchini, mushrooms, onion, garlic, and peppers and sauté, covered, for 3 minutes. Drain off excess liquid. (Save the liquid; it makes a great stock for soups and stews.) Allow vegetables to cool.

Mix in tofu, parsley, oregano, cumin, salt and pepper, basil, optional syrup, wheat germ, stuffing mix, and tomato. Add refried beans or (if cooking in a fry pan) just enough flour to make mixture easy to handle.

Make 8 patties. Grill (using a grilling basket) until just lightly browned on both sides. Serve on sesame buns.

★ SERVES 8

Banana Butternutters

• •

A burger with bananas? Trust us, it works. Our thanks to Nita Norman of Etna, New Hampshire, for a unique blend of ingredients that produces a super burger. Baked fresh butternut squash works best in this recipe.

1½ cups cooked mashed butternut squash
1½ cups cooked brown rice
1 medium banana, mashed
1 tablespoon chopped parsley
2 tablespoons minced onion
¼ cup chopped pecans
¼ cup chopped celery
2 cups dry bread crumbs
¼ teaspoon coriander
Salt and pepper to taste

Mix all of the ingredients and form into 10 medium patties. Cook on well-oiled grill.

★ SERVES 5

Mexicali Burger

. . . .

The following recipe was adapted from one contributed by Truda
Weaver of Norwalk, Connecticut. We made it a bit more south-of-the-
border by adding chili powder and changing some of the vegetables.
That's the great thing about veggie burgers: They can be easily
adapted to any cuisine, just by changing a few ingredients.

2 cups cooked brown rice
2 cups cooked pinto beans or black beans (about 1 and ½
    cans of canned beans)
1 cup dried rolled oats
½ cup finely shredded carrots
½ cup finely chopped red pepper
½ cup corn kernels
⅓ cup sunflower seeds
1 garlic clove, peeled and minced
3 tablespoons salsa
3 tablespoons fresh chopped coriander
½ teaspoon chili powder
½ teaspoon cumin
¼ teaspoon salt
8 soft tortillas (optional)
Chopped sweet onions (optional)
Slices of avocado (optional)

Combine rice, beans, rolled oats, and carrots in a food processor
and pulse to a uniform coarse-grained texture. Add the remaining
ingredients, mix well, and shape into 8 patties, using about ½ cup
mixture for each.

If you want to serve these burgers in a soft tortilla, shape them
into 8 long narrow patties. Place in a grilling basket and grill about 5

minutes on each side or until brown. Top with chopped sweet onions, several slices of avocado, and more salsa to taste.

★ SERVES 8

Armenian Burgers

• •

This burger recipe, sent in by Irene Katib of Fort Myers Beach, Florida, originally called for fava beans. Unfortunately, except for the canned variety, fava beans are difficult to find in the United States. We've substituted chickpeas (garbanzo beans). The flavor of these burgers is intriguing, hot spiciness from the cayenne and a refreshing coolness from the mint. The texture, too, is unusual, almost nutty, as the garbanzo beans are cooked only for a short time.

> *2 cups dried garbanzo beans, OR 1 cup dried garbanzo*
> *beans and 1 cup dried fava beans*
> *½ cup chopped onion*
> *¼ cup plus 1 tablespoon olive oil*
> *One 16-ounce can vegetarian refried beans*
> *1 cup stuffing mix, crushed fine*
> *1 teaspoon each onion powder and garlic powder*
> *½ cup chopped parsley*
> *¼ cup dried crushed mint*
> *½ teaspoon each cayenne, cumin powder, and salt*

Boil the beans in water to cover for 10 minutes. Turn off the heat and let stand for 2 to 3 hours in the hot water. Drain the beans and grind in a food processor until fine.

Sauté the onion in 1 tablespoon olive oil.

Mix all of the ingredients until well blended. Shape into 12 patties and grill until lightly browned.

★ MAKES 12 BURGERS

On the Grill: Burgers and Other Grillables   **31**

Garden Medley Vegetable Burgers

. . . .

These fabulous burgers, a recipe of Elinor Mink's from Fair Haven, New Jersey, are like a glorified potato cake. To make them firmer for outdoor grilling we add ½ cup bread crumbs or stuffing mix. They are truly a meal in one, with their unusual combination of potatoes, beans, fruit, and vegetables. Don't let the long list of ingredients deter you; these burgers are well worth the effort!

4 large cloves garlic, peeled and minced
1 cup yellow onion, peeled and chopped
3 tablespoons olive oil
¾ pound potatoes, boiled, drained, and mashed OR 1⅓
    cups made from instant potato flakes
1 cup cooked Great Northern Beans
½ cup crumb stuffing mix or fine dry bread crumbs (the
    crumbs will make the mixture stiffer if you plan to use
    an outdoor grill; you may want to omit them if cooking
    on a skillet indoors)
¼ cup applesauce
¼ cup chunky peanut butter
1 teaspoon coarse black pepper
4 teaspoons fresh minced ginger
¼ cup each chopped parsley and chopped cilantro
2 teaspoons sesame seeds
1 teaspoon ground cumin
½ teaspoon whole cumin seeds (optional)
½ cup each: frozen green peas, chopped red pepper, chopped
    carrots, chopped green beans, chopped cauliflower
Salt to taste

Sauté garlic and onions in olive oil until soft. Add to mashed potatoes.

Rinse and drain beans, and add beans and stuffing to potato mixture. Add applesauce, peanut butter, pepper, ginger, herbs, sesame seeds, and cumin. Stir gently until blended.

Steam the five vegetables together for 3 minutes. Shock with cold water and drain. Gently fold into potato/bean mixture. Add stuffing mix and combine thoroughly. Add salt if desired.

Form into 8 patties. Chill in refrigerator for several hours. Place in a grilling basket and grill until lightly browned.

★ MAKES 8 BURGERS

Mock Crab Cakes

• •

These croquettes are always popular in the cooking classes of local Seventh-Day Adventist churches. The traditional recipe calls for eggs, but we've created a cholesterol-free version using a wonderful egg substitute made from flax seeds.

3 tablespoons flax seeds
½ cup water
2½ cups shredded zucchini
1 ounce soft tofu, blended
2 cups dry bread crumbs
1 teaspoon Angostura low-sodium Worcestershire sauce
1½ tablespoons Old Bay seasoning
2 tablespoons flour

In a blender, grind the flax seeds into a fine powder. Add the water and blend until a mixture with the consistency of egg whites forms (about 1 minute).

Mix this with all remaining ingredients and press into 6 cakes. Grill on an oiled screen over hot coals.

★ SERVES 6

Walnut Oat Burgers with Apricots

Dried apricots give this burger a pleasant hint of sweetness; chunks of green peppers give it a cheerful crunch. It's adapted from the favorite family burger recipe of Carolyn Albert of Brooklyn Heights, New York.

> 1 medium onion, peeled and coarsely chopped
> 1 medium green pepper, cored, seeded, and coarsely
>   chopped
> ½ cup minced fresh parsley
> 1 pound soft tofu
> 3 tablespoons soy sauce
> ½ tablespoon Dijon mustard
> ½ teaspoon garlic powder
> ½ cup chopped walnuts
> 1 cup quick oats, uncooked
> ½ cup fresh cubed bread crumbs
> 15 dried apricot halves, coarsely chopped

Place the onion in a saucepan and cover with boiling water. Simmer for 3 minutes and drain. Combine the onion, pepper, and parsley.

Drain the tofu and squeeze in a paper towel to remove excess water. Mash tofu with a fork. Add to onion mixture and blend. Mix in remaining ingredients. Refrigerate for ½ hour.

Form into 8 patties and grill until browned on both sides.

★ SERVES 8

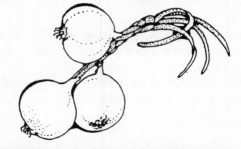

Green Goddess Burger

. . . .

This burger from Gwen Lawrence of Media, Pennsylvania, has a pleasant crunchy texture. The various tastes blend subtly and we find that they hold together well on the grill. If you don't have any cooked brown rice on hand, try instant brown rice, which can be ready in 10 minutes. Serve in a whole-wheat pita, and top with additional slices of avocado and juicy fresh tomatoes. The burgers are delicious as leftovers, served at room temperature as a sandwich filling.

2 tablespoons sesame seeds
2 tablespoons sunflower seeds
½ cup oatmeal
½ cup cooked brown rice
½ cup cooked lentils
½ cup cooked beans, such as white navy beans
½ cup minced onions
½ cup fine dry bread crumbs or crumb stuffing mix
2 tablespoons chopped pecans
¼ cup chopped fresh parsley
½ teaspoon Italian herb blend, or 1 teaspoon fresh herbs
1 tablespoon each tomato purée and tahini
⅓ cup chopped fresh mushrooms
½ sliced avocado, chopped
Additional avocado slices, for garnish
Sliced tomatoes, for garnish

Process the sesame seeds and sunflower seeds in a blender, add the oatmeal and process until ground. Mix with remaining ingredients except garnishes and shape into 8 patties. Grill until browned on both sides.

★ SERVES 8

Grilled Five-Spice Tofu

. . . .

This simple marinade produces a tofu dish with an exquisite flavor. Look for Chinese five-spice powder in Asian markets or natural foods stores. Curry paste is sold in specialty stores, including Asian and Indian markets.

> *1 pound extra-firm tofu*
> *⅓ cup soy sauce*
> *1 tablespoon water*
> *1 tablespoon maple syrup*
> *1 tablespoon minced fresh ginger root*
> *1 teaspoon curry powder, or 1 tablespoon Patak-brand*
>   *curry paste*
> *½ teaspoon Chinese five-spice powder*

Cut the tofu into 8 pieces. Whisk together remaining ingredients and pour over tofu. Let marinate, refrigerated, for at least 1 hour.

Grill over hot coals, turning frequently and basting with marinade, until the tofu is browned and completely heated through. Serve in rolls.

This dish can also be baked inside. Bake in a casserole dish at 350 degrees for 30 minutes, covered; then uncover and bake for an additional 20 minutes.

★ SERVES 4

Sweet and Tangy Barbecue Sauce

. . . .

A super barbecue sauce that is delicious on tofu or tempeh, grilled onions, potatoes, or vegetable shish kebabs.

3 tablespoons vegetable oil
½ cup cider vinegar
¾ cup catsup
¼ cup Angostura reduced-sodium Worcestershire sauce
5 tablespoons brown sugar
1 teaspoon salt

Combine all ingredients in a saucepan and bring to a boil. Lower heat and simmer for 5 minutes. Keeps refrigerated for up to three weeks.

★ SERVES 12

ℬutter ℬean ℬarley ℬulgur ℬurger

• •

Barley and bulgur give this burger a lovely chewy quality and a familiar burger texture. If you prefer, use 1½ cups cooked barley and skip the bulgur (but then it won't be as much fun to say its name).

1 cup cooked or canned butter beans
¾ cup cooked barley
¾ cup cooked bulgur
½ cup quick oatmeal, uncooked
1½ tablespoons soy sauce
1 teaspoon dried basil
1 stalk celery, chopped
1 small onion, peeled and chopped
1 clove garlic, peeled and finely minced

With a fork or potato masher, mash the butter beans just slightly. They should be chunky, not puréed. Add the rest of the ingredients and form into 6 patties. Grill until browned on each side.

★ SERVES 6

Vegetable Garden Burger

• • • • • • • • • • • • • • • • • • • •

Enjoy the exquisite taste of fresh summer vegetables in this burger
from Claire McIntosh of Brooklyn, New York.

*1 medium eggplant, unpeeled, sliced crosswise into six ¾-
inch slices*
1 large Bermuda onion, peeled and sliced into 6 disks
1 large zucchini squash, sliced lengthwise into 6 strips
*1 large yellow summer squash, sliced lengthwise into 6
strips*
Six ½-inch slices of beefsteak tomato
Six Kaiser rolls

❦ MARINADE
¾ cup virgin olive oil
3 cloves garlic, peeled and crushed
1 tablespoon chopped parsley
1 tablespoon crushed basil
1 tablespoon oregano
1 tablespoon rosemary
1 teaspoon thyme
6 ounces V-8 juice
⅓ cup herb-flavored vinegar (such as tarragon vinegar)
Celery salt

Combine marinade ingredients in a large bowl. Marinate the vegetables
in the marinade for at least 2 hours.

Grill vegetables on both sides over medium hot coals until they
are tender and slightly charred. Slice the rolls and lightly grill on both
sides.

Place a slice of eggplant on one half of the Kaiser roll. Follow with slices of onion, zucchini, yellow summer squash and tomato. Sprinkle the tomato with celery salt and top with the other half of the bun.

★ 6 SERVINGS

P-nutty Garden Burgers with Sunny Relish

• • • • • • • • • • • • • • • • • • •

Helen Conwell of Fairhope, Alabama, created a burger with a lovely crunch and an exotic mango sauce.

¾ cup *Wheatena-brand cereal*
1½ cups *water*
¾ teaspoon *salt*
½ cup *raisins*
¼ cup *smooth peanut butter*
½ cup *chopped celery*
2 cups *shredded carrots*
½ medium *onion, peeled and chopped*
½ cup *finely chopped dry-roasted peanuts*

❦ **SUNNY RELISH**
1 cup *mango chutney*
¼ cup *bottled chili sauce*

Mix the cereal, water, and salt and simmer for 10 minutes. Stir in raisins, peanut butter, celery, carrots, and onion.

Mix the relish ingredients and set aside.

Form the burger mix into 8 patties and dip in the chopped peanuts. Grill until browned on both sides. Serve with Sunny Relish.

★ SERVES 8

Papagalos Veggie Burgers

• •

Marshall and Litza Monsell, who own the Papagalos Restaurant in Naxos, Greece, created this delicious burger. They comment that it's the number one favorite at their restaurant and, although a "bit of work, is well worth it!" Its interesting combination of spices and seasonings gives it an intriguing flavor. Papagalos usually serves the burger with a teriyaki or marsala sauce.

½ cup dry chickpeas
½ cup dry yellow lentils
¼ cup brown lentils
¼ cup catsup
1½ tablespoons tomato paste
1 tablespoon Angostura-brand low-sodium Worcestershire sauce
2 tablespoons toasted sesame seeds
1 medium onion, peeled and minced
1 large carrot, peeled and minced
1 tablespoon curry powder
1½ teaspoons oregano
1 teaspoon each cumin and dried ginger
¼ teaspoon coriander
¼ packet taco seasoning mix
1 tablespoon dried mint
Salt and pepper to taste
1 cup flour

Soak chickpeas and both kinds of lentils overnight in water to cover. Drain in the morning. Set aside about ¼ of the soaked chickpeas. Put the remaining chickpeas and the yellow lentils in enough water to cover and boil for 15 to 20 minutes. Drain and process in food processor until a medium smooth texture is attained. Add catsup, tomato paste, Worcestershire, and sesame seeds.

In another pot, brown the onion and carrot until just barely tender; set aside.

Mix brown lentils and curry powder, add just enough water to cover, and cook for 15 to 20 minutes. Don't drain, but blend in a blender to a creamy texture.

Put in a large bowl all the remaining spices, the carrots and onions, processed chickpeas, yellow lentils, and salt and pepper. Mix well and add flour to attain a doughy consistency, then add brown lentils and mix again.

In a food processor, coarsely chop the reserved chickpeas and add those to the mixture. Let stand in refrigerator for 2 hours or so to thicken. Shape into 8 burgers and grill until browned on both sides.

★ SERVES 8

Yamburgers

• •

A burger with the taste of autumn, this is a wonderful choice for an end-of-the-season cookout.

2 medium-sized yams
2 tablespoons margarine
½ cup chopped walnuts
2 cups dry crumb stuffing mix
¼ cup chopped celery
¼ cup minced onion
¼ cup raisins

Bake or boil the yams until tender. Peel and mash. Mix all of the ingredients together and form into 6 patties. Grill until nicely browned on both sides.

★ SERVES 6

Elaine's Burger

. . . .

Elaine French, president of the Vegetarian Society of Honolulu, offers this patty with real old-fashioned burger flavor. TVP is texturized vegetable protein, a soy protein product with a meaty texture. Look for it in natural foods stores.

> *1 cup TVP*
> *½ medium onion, peeled and finely chopped*
> *4 ounces fresh mushrooms, finely chopped*
> *¼ cup cornmeal*
> *¼ cup quick oats*
> *2 tablespoons nutritional yeast*
> *1 tablespoon flour*
> *½ teaspoon cumin*
> *¼ teaspoon black pepper*
> *¼ cup A-1 sauce*
> *1 tablespoon Angostura low-sodium Worcestershire sauce*

Boil a scant cup water and pour over the TVP. Set aside.

Simmer the onion and mushrooms in ¼ cup water until they are tender and all the excess liquid from the mushrooms has evaporated.

In a large bowl, combine the cornmeal, oats, yeast, flour, cumin, and pepper and mix well. Add the A-1 sauce and the Worcestershire sauce to the TVP and stir until combined. Then stir this mixture into the large bowl of dry ingredients along with the onion-mushroom mixture.

Form into 8 patties and grill for 3 to 4 minutes on each side, using a grilling screen lightly brushed with oil.

★ MAKES 8 BURGERS

Cajun Grills

. . . .

These easy-to-fix burgers, with a pleasant chewiness, can readily be adapted to any type of cuisine with the addition of various spices. Susan Asanovic of Wilton, Connecticut, submitted the Cajun Grills. We experimented with the basic recipe and came up with the Mideast Grill.

12 ounces tempeh

1 medium onion, peeled and finely chopped

2 cloves garlic, peeled and finely chopped

½ teaspoon each: garlic powder, ground black pepper,
ground white pepper, dried thyme

1 teaspoon dried oregano

¼ teaspoon cayenne

2 tablespoons tomato paste

2 tablespoons flour

1 to 2 tablespoons barbecue sauce

1 tablespoon lemon juice

Salt to taste

Mild vegetable oil, for coating

Grind tempeh, preferably in a food grinder, but a food processor will do; be careful not to make a paste. Combine with remaining ingredients and shape into 4 patties.

Coat very lightly with mild vegetable oil and grill slowly on both sides until browned, turning once. Served with salsa, relish, and a dash of Pickapeppa Sauce if you like.

★ SERVES 4

Mideast Grills

. . . .

Follow the above recipe, omitting the barbecue sauce, oregano, and thyme. Instead add:

1 teaspoon each: cumin seeds and dried mint
¼ teaspoon cinnamon
½ teaspoon salt
2 tablespoons raisins
1 tablespoon sunflower seeds

★ SERVES 4

Grilled Tempeh

. . . .

Celeste Wyatt of Holiday, Florida, sent us this recipe for tempeh burgers. Tempeh, a fermented soy product, has an interesting, slightly crunchy texture, soaks up marinade nicely, and holds up well on the grill. You can either cut the tempeh into 3-inch squares and serve in a regular whole wheat hamburger bun, or cut it in smaller 1-inch pieces and skewer along with marinated mushrooms, onion wedges, and cherry tomatoes.

❦ **MARINADE**
2 cloves garlic, peeled and crushed
3 tablespoons tamari or low-sodium soy sauce
3 tablespoons sherry or Madeira
1 tablespoon lemon juice
1 teaspoon each snipped fresh rosemary and fresh tarragon
*   (½ teaspoon each dried)*
¼ cup olive oil

One 8-ounce package of tempeh will serve 4 people as a kebab with additional vegetables. Use 2 packages if you plan to serve the tempeh as a burger.

Cut tempeh into 3-inch squares or 1-inch pieces and marinate for at least 1 hour. If you plan to skewer the tempeh, add mushrooms to the marinade. Grill until nicely brown, brushing with the marinade. You can pop the whole kebab in a toasted French roll.

Tempeh with Apricot Marinade

• • • • • • • • • • • • • • • • • • •

Fruit preserves make wonderful barbecue sauces and marinades. The sweetness of apricots makes them a perfect companion for the more smoky, earthy flavor of tempeh, a staple of Indonesian cooking.

1 pound tempeh
1 cup apricot preserves
1 clove garlic, peeled and minced
2 tablespoons oil
¼ cup soy sauce
2 tablespoons cider vinegar

Cut the tempeh into 2-inch squares. Place in a vegetable steamer and steam for 20 minutes.

Combine the apricot preserves, garlic, oil, soy sauce, and vinegar and mix thoroughly. Place the steamed tempeh in a large bowl and pour the apricot marinade over it. Marinate in the refrigerator for an hour.

Grill, brushing frequently with the marinade and turning the tempeh pieces every few minutes, until tempeh is browned and completely heated through. Serve on rolls or over rice.

★ SERVES 8

Best Veggie Burger

. . . .

Rhea Gendizier of Lexington, Massachusetts, makes a burger that adds the tang of a Granny Smith apple to the wonderful crunch of fresh vegetables.

¼ pound green beans
½ cup cracked wheat
1 small zucchini
1 small carrot
½ Granny Smith apple, peeled
½ cup cooked or canned chickpeas
1 tablespoon minced onion
1 clove garlic, peeled
1 tablespoon sesame tahini or peanut butter
½ teaspoon curry powder
½ teaspoon chili powder
½ teaspoon salt
Black pepper to taste
1½ tablespoons canola oil
½ cup dry bread crumbs

Cook the green beans in boiling water until tender-crisp. Drain and chop fine.

Cook cracked wheat in 1 cup boiling water for 1 minute. Remove from heat and cover.

Grate the zucchini, carrot, and apple, and combine with the chopped beans.

In a food processor blend chickpeas, onion, garlic, tahini, curry powder, chili powder, salt, pepper, and canola oil until smooth. Add to vegetables.

Drain cracked wheat into strainer, pressing with back of spoon to extract excess liquid. Add to bowl with vegetables. Add bread crumbs. Refrigerate for 1 hour.

Shape into 6 burgers. Cook 3 minutes on each side on grill lightly brushed with oil.

★ SERVES 6

Tofu Nut Burgers

• •

These delicious burgers, submitted by Shari Goodman of Santa Ana, California, are quick and easy to make.

> *1 clove garlic, peeled and minced*
> *½ cup chopped onion*
> *½ cup finely chopped celery*
> *1 teaspoon olive oil*
> *¼ cup barbecue sauce*
> *¼ cup low-sodium soy sauce*
> *¾ cup soft silken tofu*
> *2 tablespoons tahini*
> *Pepper to taste*
> *2 cups finely chopped almonds*
> *2 cups crumb stuffing mix*

Sauté garlic, onion, and celery in olive oil. Set aside to cool.

In a mixing bowl combine barbecue sauce, soy sauce, tofu, tahini, and pepper. Blend well and add onion mixture and almonds. Mix well and then add the stuffing mix.

Shape into 8 patties and grill about 3 to 4 minutes on a side.

★ SERVES 8

Mesquite-flavored Kebabs

. . . .

Adding mesquite chips to your barbecue coals gives these kebabs a unique flavor. Any combination of fresh vegetables will do, but be sure to include mushrooms. Partially baked elephant head garlic, which is extra large but extra mild, is a wonderful addition.

8 large brown mushroom caps

8 firm cherry tomatoes

8 wedges of peeled sweet onions

4 to 8 peeled cloves elephant head garlic, baked at least 25 minutes

1 cup mesquite chips for coals

❦ **MARINADE**

3 tablespoons olive oil

1 teaspoon Dijon mustard

1 tablespoon sherry or wine vinegar

2 tablespoons Salsa Verde (see page 80)

½ teaspoon chili powder

❦ **GARNISH (OPTIONAL)**

1 cup coarsely chopped corn chips

¼ cup cilantro leaves

½ cup Salsa Verde (page 80)

Mix the marinade ingredients together and pour over vegetables. Marinate in the refrigerator for at least an hour.

While vegetables are marinating, soak the mesquite chips in water for several minutes. When the coals are very hot (covered in white ash), drain the mesquite chips and toss over coals.

Arrange the vegetables on skewers and place the kebabs over the coals and, to get the most flavor, cover the grill. (If your grill has no cover, use aluminum foil). Grill until browned, turning once or twice and brushing with marinade. Garnish with corn chips, cilantro, and a dollop of Salsa Verde, if you like.

★ SERVES 4

Grilled Tofu with Korean Barbecue Sauce

· ·

The sweet-and-salty flavor of Korean barbecue sauce is a perfect accompaniment to the delicate flavor of tofu. This is a fast and easy grilled entrée.

1 pound firm tofu
1 tablespoon toasted sesame seeds
3 green onions, tops and bulbs chopped
4 cloves garlic, peeled and minced
¼ cup soy sauce
2 tablespoons sesame oil
2 tablespoons maple syrup
2 tablespoons sherry
⅛ teaspoon pepper

Press the tofu in paper towels to squeeze out excess water. Cut tofu in 2-inch cubes.

In a large bowl, mix the remaining ingredients. Toss with the tofu and allow to marinate, refrigerated, for several hours.

Grill, basting with the extra marinade until tofu is browned. Serve over rice or in pita pockets.

★ SERVES 4

On the Grill: Burgers and Other Grillables

Vegetable Kebabs with Lemony Marinade

• •

This is a simple marinade that goes well on almost any grilled item. Try it on these vegetable shish kebabs. These are wonderful served over rice.

 4 medium potatoes, unpeeled, cut into 6 chunks each
 2 medium carrots, peeled and cut into 4 chunks each
 2 small onions, peeled and quartered
 1 medium zucchini, cut into 8 chunks
 8 mushrooms
 8 cherry tomatoes

❧ **MARINADE**
 ¼ cup olive oil
 Juice of ½ lemon
 Thyme
 Pepper

Steam the potatoes and carrots for 7 or 8 minutes, until almost tender. Place them in a bowl with the rest of the vegetables.

Combine marinade ingredients in a jar and shake well. Pour over vegetables and let marinate in the refrigerator for at least 2 hours.

Arrange vegetables on 8 skewers and grill over hot coals, turning frequently, until all vegetables are tender and slightly charred.

★ SERVES 8

Sweet Potato Kebabs with Rosemary and Lime Marinade

• •

Fresh lime juice is one of the loveliest flavors of summer. Try this special marinade on eggplant or zucchini or any favorite shish kebab like the sweet potato version we offer here.

3 large sweet potatoes
2 large white potatoes
8 mushrooms
1 red pepper, seeded, cored, and cut into chunks
2 cups firm tofu, cut into large chunks

❦ **MARINADE**
1 teaspoon Dijon mustard
1 clove garlic, peeled and pressed
2 tablespoons maple syrup
2 tablespoons low-sodium soy sauce
1 to 2 tablespoons fresh squeezed lime juice
1 to 2 tablespoons finely snipped fresh rosemary, or 2
    teaspoons dry, crushed rosemary
2 tablespoons olive oil
Freshly ground black pepper

Steam or boil the sweet potatoes and the white potatoes until both are just barely tender. Allow to cool slightly and then peel them. Place them in a bowl with the mushrooms, pepper, and tofu.

Combine all marinade ingredients and pour over vegetables and tofu. Let vegetables marinate at least 1 hour.

Arrange on skewers and grill, turning frequently, until browned and tender.

★ SERVES 8

Tofu Corn Puff Burger

. . . .

Light and fluffy, with an indescribably rich flavor, these delicate croquettes must be cooked in a grilling basket or on a grilling screen.

½ cup cashews
½ cup water
½ pound tofu
½ small onion, peeled and finely chopped
2 tablespoons nutritional yeast
2 cups frozen corn, defrosted and cooked
2 tablespoons chopped fresh basil
2 cups fresh cubed bread crumbs
Salt and pepper to taste

Blend the cashews and water in a blender or food processor for 1 minute or so until completely puréed. Add the tofu and blend until smooth. Transfer to a bowl and mix in the remaining ingredients.

Form 8 patties and grill in a basket or on a grilling screen on both sides until browned.

★ SERVES 8

Grilled Potatoes with Rosemary

. . . .

Potatoes are such a hearty and filling food, why not serve a big platter of them as an entrée? Dusted with rosemary and grilled to a golden crunch, these are easy and delicious.

4 large baking potatoes
1 tablespoon olive oil
3 tablespoons minced shallots

1 tablespoon dried rosemary
1 teaspoon balsamic vinegar
Salt and pepper to taste

Slice the potatoes lengthwise, producing 6 slices per potato.

Whisk together the olive oil, shallots, rosemary, vinegar, and salt and pepper. Brush the potato slices with this mixture. Grill, turning frequently, until browned and tender.

★ SERVES 4

Minted Grilled Zucchini and Carrots

• •

The assertive flavor and aroma of fresh mint is a perfect match for blander vegetables like zucchini and carrots. This is a wonderful grilled side dish that looks beautiful and tastes magical.

3 medium carrots, sliced lengthwise in ½-inch-thick slices
3 small zucchini, sliced lengthwise in ½-inch-thick slices
½ teaspoon Dijon mustard
3 tablespoons chopped fresh mint
1 tablespoon chopped parsley
3 tablespoons olive oil
Salt and pepper to taste

Steam the carrots for 10 minutes, until barely tender. Whisk together the mustard, mint, parsley, olive oil, and salt and pepper. Brush the carrot and zucchini slices with this mixture and place on a hot grill. Grill, turning frequently, until vegetables are tender and slightly charred on the outside.

★ SERVES 4

Vegetables on the Grill

· ·

Almost any vegetable goes on the grill. Try several of the following and serve them arranged on a big platter, with fresh bread and a salad or two for a super, healthy cookout. The Sweet and Tangy Barbecue Sauce that follows these instructions for grilling vegetables is especially delicious on onions and potatoes. Or you may want to try the marinades from the recipes for Vegetable Kebabs on page 50 or for Sweet Potato Kebabs on page 51.

Carrots: Scrub whole small or medium-sized carrots. Brush with a little olive oil and dust with dried herbs. Place toward edges of the grill rather than directly over the coals. Cook for 15 to 20 minutes, turning frequently.

Corn: Traditionally, corn is cooked right in its husk; you can also cook it wrapped in aluminum foil.
In the husk: Bend the leaves back and gently remove the silk. Fold the leaves back into place and tie them together with a thin strip of corn husk. Place corn directly over the coals, about 4 to 5 inches away from the fire. Cook for a total of 15 minutes, turning every 5 minutes or so.
Foil-wrapped: Remove husks and silk. Wrap in aluminum foil, twisting the ends. Grill as for corn in the husk.

Mushrooms: Mushrooms, with their earthy flavor, are just made for the grill. Since they are small and can get a little "floppy" on the grill, they are best cooked on skewers. Brush them with just a bit of olive oil if desired and dust with herbs of your choice. Cook over coals until just tender.

Barbecued Onions: Marinate onions in a barbecue sauce for several hours, then cook over a medium fire for 3 minutes on each side.

Potatoes: Whole potatoes can be baked right in the coals. Bury them in the coals and cook for 45 minutes or so. The skins become blackened and are not edible, but the insides will be tender and delicious. Alternatively, you can wrap them well in foil first, which helps to preserve the skins.

Small new potatoes can be cooked on a skewer (metal skewers will speed the cooking time). Rub the potatoes with olive oil first and begin to cook them near the edge of the fire. Rotate the skewers every 5 minutes or so, gradually moving them toward the center of the grill, directly over the coals. Serve the potatoes with a sprinkle of rosemary, dill, or chives. For faster cooking, steam the potatoes first until barely tender. Then skewer and grill until browned.

Summer Squash: All of the summer squashes can be cooked on the grill. Try patty pan, zucchini, or crookneck. Slice the squash into ½-inch slices. If using zucchini, the most popular kind for grilling, slice them lengthwise. Brush with olive oil and sprinkle with salt and a little basil or oregano. Grill until just tender, about 4 to 5 minutes on each side.

Sweet Potatoes: Sweet potatoes can be cooked on the grill in the same manner as white potatoes, but they are best when buried in the coals and baked. Don't wrap them in foil; just scrub and then bury completely—don't just toss them on top of the coals. It will take close to an hour for the potatoes to become thoroughly cooked and tender. The skins will be completely charred and can't be eaten, but the flesh will be sweet and delicious. Serve them with a little margarine and brown sugar, or for a different taste sensation, a few drops of fresh lime juice and a sprinkle of salt and fresh herbs.

On the Grill: Burgers and Other Grillables

CHAPTER FOUR

Dips, Salads, and Side Dishes

I f burgers and vegetable steaks are the heart of the barbecue, salads and side dishes can be the most popular items at the party. We've included a few old-fashioned picnic favorites like potato and macaroni salads, and baked beans, but we've dressed them up and slimmed them down a bit. Our salads use a wonderful cholesterol-free mayonnaise made from sweet silken tofu blended with one of summer's best flavors—fresh basil. And our baked bean recipe shuns fatty chunks of pork in favor of the spiciness of ginger and other spices. We've also introduced some new tastes to put some fun in your picnics. Try Jicama Salad with Mint and Oranges, or New Zealand Kiwi and Brown Rice Salad. For a little extra fire at your picnic, serve Watermelon Fire and Ice Salsa, or Salsa Verde. Or you might want to forgo those little plastic forks in favor of finger food like Nori Rolls or Stuffed Grape Leaves.

Eggplant Dip

• •

Irma Laskey of Denville, New Jersey, offers this super party dip. It should be made ahead and refrigerated for 24 hours to allow the flavors to mingle. Serve it with crackers, pita wedges, or squares of rye bread.

> 2 medium eggplants
> 4 cloves garlic, peeled and thinly sliced
> 1 teaspoon soy sauce
> 2 tablespoons olive oil
> 1 medium tomato, finely chopped
> 2 tablespoons lemon juice
> ¼ cup golden raisins
> ½ cup finely chopped onions
> ¼ cup chopped parsley
> 4 teaspoons sugar
> ¼ cup toasted pine nuts

Cut the eggplants in half lengthwise and then make deep slits in the flesh. Insert garlic slices in slits. Bake on a cookie sheet at 350 degrees for 1 hour.

Scrape the eggplant flesh into a bowl and mash with a fork. Add remaining ingredients except for pine nuts, and mix well. Cover and refrigerate. Add pine nuts just before serving.

★ SERVES 12

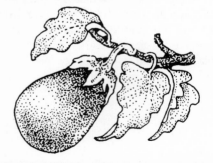

White Bean Dip with Lemon and Garlic

• • • • • • • • • • • • • • • • • • •

The lemon zest adds an appealing fresh taste to this dip. Zesters, small, rakelike utensils that remove just the yellow part of the rind, can be purchased in most cooking supply shops.

3 cups cooked white, navy or cannellini beans
1 tablespoon olive oil (optional)
Zest of 1 lemon (scrape off the zest before you squeeze the juice)
Juice of 1 lemon
2 or 3 cloves garlic, peeled and minced or pressed through garlic press
Dash of cayenne or hot sauce
¼ teaspoon salt (optional)
3 tablespoons chopped chives

In a blender or food processor, process the beans, olive oil, lemon zest, lemon juice, garlic, cayenne, and salt (optional) until smooth. Transfer to a medium bowl and add chopped chives. May be served at room temperature or chilled.

★ SERVES 6

Nasturtiums Filled with Guacamole

. . . .

This is one of the prettiest appetizers possible. It was created by Susan Belsinger, whose book, *Flowers in the Kitchen*, is one of the loveliest and most unusual cookbooks we have come across. You'll need to grow your own nasturtiums, but it is easy to do. If you don't have a garden, grow them in small pots on the window sill. Both the flowers and leaves, which have a spicy pepperiness, are wonderful in salads. The jicama provides a nice crunchy base. If you don't have jicama, Jerusalem artichokes are a good substitute.

1 large ripe avocado
2 teaspoons lime juice, plus additional for the jicama
1 small ripe tomato, very finely chopped
2 tablespoons finely minced onion
1 jalapeño or serrano chile, seeded and finely minced
1 small clove garlic, peeled and finely minced
Salt
About 20 nasturtium blossoms
1 small jicama

Peel the avocado and remove the pit. Mash the avocado in a bowl with a fork and add the lime juice. Blend in the tomato, onion, chile, and garlic. Add salt to taste. Let the guacamole stand, covered, while preparing the nasturtiums and jicama.

Rinse the nasturtium blossoms carefully and pat them dry. Peel the jicama and slice it about ¼ inch thick. Cut the slices into pieces about 2 by 2 inches. They don't have to be perfect squares—leave the rounded edges. They should be just the right size to accommodate a nasturtium filled with guacamole. Squeeze a little lime juice over the jicama slices.

At this point, the guacamole, jicama, and nasturtiums can be kept for a few hours in the refrigerator, if necessary. Then assemble the appetizers: Hold the nasturtium blossoms at the base and use a teaspoon to fill them carefully with the guacamole. Set each filled nasturtium on a slice of jicama and arrange on a serving platter. The prepared appetizers can be kept very briefly in the refrigerator or served immediately.

★ ABOUT 20 APPETIZERS

$\mathcal{D}$illed Chickpeas

· ·

This is one of the most irresistible salads we've ever tasted. Be certain to use fresh dill, and serve the salad at room temperature for maximum flavor.

1 carrot, sliced
1 potato, peeled and diced
One 16-ounce can chickpeas (or 2 cups cooked)
½ cup shelled fresh peas, or frozen peas, thawed
1 large onion, peeled and thinly sliced
2 cloves garlic, peeled and crushed
1 tablespoon olive oil
1 tablespoon balsamic vinegar
1 tablespoon raspberry vinegar
2 tablespoons snipped fresh dill
Salt and pepper to taste

Place the sliced carrot in 1 cup of water and simmer for 5 minutes. Add the diced potato and cook for another 10 minutes. Remove pan from heat and drain any excess liquid. Add the chickpeas and peas to the other vegetables and toss to warm them.

Sauté onion and garlic in the oil until tender. Add onion, garlic, balsamic and raspberry vinegar, and dill to chickpea mixture. Toss to combine. Add salt and pepper to taste. Serve at room temperature.

★ SERVES 6

New Zealand Brown Rice and Kiwi Salad

· ·

This is a wonderful salad that combines the crunch of fresh raw vegetables with the tangy sweetness of kiwi and Granny Smith apples.

2 kiwi fruit
1 Granny Smith apple
3 cups cooked brown rice
½ cup thinly sliced celery
½ cup sweet red pepper strips
¼ cup toasted walnut or pecan pieces
¼ cup thinly sliced green onions
2 teaspoons dried mint
2 tablespoons chopped fresh parsley
3 tablespoons sherry vinegar
1 tablespoon olive oil

Peel the kiwi and cut into ¼-inch slices. Cut slices in half to form half circles. Core and dice apple into ½-inch cubes. Toss together rice, kiwi, apple, celery, red pepper strips, nuts, green onions, mint, and parsley in a bowl.

In a separate bowl, mix together the vinegar and oil; drizzle over salad. Toss well. Cover and refrigerate 1 to 2 hours to allow flavors to blend.

★ SERVES 8

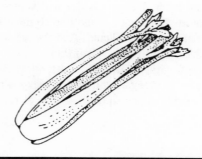

Lentil Confetti Salad

• •

This is a pretty salad to dress up your picnic table.

½ cup lentils, rinsed and drained
1½ cups water
1 cup cooked rice
1 teaspoon salt
1 small tomato, diced
½ seeded and chopped orange bell pepper
½ cup cooked corn
⅓ cup finely chopped parsley
1 teaspoon minced fresh tarragon, or ½ teaspoon dried
tarragon
¼ cup chopped onion
2 tablespoons chopped celery
2 tablespoons sliced pimiento-stuffed green olives
2 tablespoons tarragon vinegar
2 tablespoons olive oil

In saucepan, combine lentils and water. Cover and bring to boil. Reduce heat; simmer 20 minutes or until lentils are tender. Drain.

Meanwhile, in a bowl, combine remaining ingredients except vinegar and oil. Add lentils, vinegar, and olive oil. Toss and chill.

★ SERVES 6

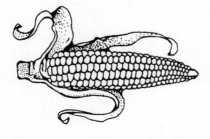

Orange and Black-eyed Pea Salad

. . . .

Fresh herbs and slices of orange give this salad wonderful, cool summer flavors.

Two 15-ounce cans black-eyed peas, or 4 cups cooked peas
2 tablespoons oil
2 tablespoons vinegar (raspberry vinegar is especially good)
Juice and grated rind of 1 orange
½ cup chopped parsley
6 minced green onions, some green tops included
¼ cup finely sliced red onions
Small handful of fresh basil, chopped (optional)
Salt and pepper
4 oranges, peeled and divided into segments
1 large bunch of watercress, washed and dried

Rinse and drain the canned black-eyed peas.

Mix oil, vinegar, orange juice, and grated orange rind with parsley, green onions, red onions, basil, if available, and salt and pepper.

Coarsely chop the segments of 3 oranges. Add those along with the peas to the oil and vinegar mixture.

Arrange watercress on 6 plates, top with pea salad. Garnish with segments of the remaining orange.

★ SERVES 6

Pasta Apricot Salad

. . . .

Fresh apricots give this salad a refreshing sweetness. It looks beautiful served on a bed of fresh greens.

4 ounces fusilli (corkscrew) pasta
¾ pound (about 5 or 6 apricots) fresh ripe unpeeled
*   apricots, cut into quarters*
½ pound zucchini, cut into julienne strips
1 red pepper, cut into julienne strips
3 tablespoons chopped fresh basil, or 1 tablespoon dry basil

❦ FRESH APRICOT-BASIL DRESSING
2 fresh ripe unpeeled apricots, pitted
2 tablespoons white wine vinegar
1½ teaspoons sugar
¼ cup vegetable oil
1 tablespoon dry basil

Cook pasta in boiling water for 10 minutes. Drain and let cool. Combine pasta, apricots, zucchini, red pepper and basil in bowl.

To make the dressing, combine apricots, vinegar, and sugar in electric blender; blend until smooth. With motor running, slowly add the vegetable oil in a thin stream. Continue blending till dressing is thick and smooth. Stir in basil.

Pour dressing over salad and toss gently.

★ SERVES 8

Dips, Salads, and Side Dishes   **67**

Jicama Salad with Mint and Oranges

You'll want to serve this simple salad at every picnic. It is pretty, easy to make, and has an exquisite flavor.

> *1 navel orange*
> *2 cups jicama, cut into 2-inch julienne strips*
> *¼ cup chopped fresh mint, or 1 tablespoon dried*
> *½ cup orange juice*
> *Lettuce leaves*
> *Avocado slices, for garnish*

Peel orange and cut each section in half. Mix all ingredients and marinate several hours. Serve on a bed of lettuce and garnish with a few slices of avocado.

★ SERVES 6

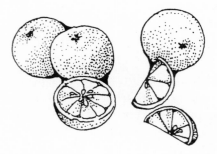

Mystery Garden Oriental Salad

Our favorite part of this salad is the dressing. We could dollop it over about anything, pasta, potatoes, rice, or veggies. No one will guess that the mysterious ingredient that gives it texture and an interesting flavor and boosts its nutritional value is toasted wheat germ! The dressing is the creation of Nina Graybill and Maxine Rapoport, authors of *The Pasta Salad Book*.

❦ **DRESSING**

½ cup toasted wheat germ, whirled until fine in a blender
¾ cup canola oil
1 teaspoon dark roasted sesame oil
½ cup lemon juice
¼ cup soy sauce
2 cloves garlic, peeled and roughly chopped

Add all the dressing ingredients to the wheat germ and process 30 seconds.

12 ounces linguine
1 tablespoon canola oil
4 green onions, most of the green tops included, sliced
   diagonally
1 cup sliced jicama, or one 8-ounce can water chestnuts,
   drained, rinsed, and sliced
1 cup fresh pea pods, crisped in ice water for at least 1
   hour, drained and patted dry
1-inch piece fresh ginger root, peeled and minced (optional)
1 small bottle baby corn, drained
½ cup chopped cilantro
Butter or Bibb lettuce

Cook pasta until al dente, drain, and toss with the oil. Mix the green onions, jicama, pea pods, ginger, baby corn, and cilantro and toss with the pasta. Serve at room temperature on a bed of butter or Bibb lettuce. Top each serving with about 2 tablespoons of the mystery dressing.

★ SERVES 8

Vegetable Rotini with Ginger Peanut Sauce

. . . .

This is a quick, easy-to-make summer salad with an unusual spicy dressing. Although the recipe calls for only broccoli and carrots, feel free to toss in more fresh vegetables, such as corn, peas, chopped jicama, or even chickpeas.

> *8 ounces rotini*
> *1 to 2 tablespoons chopped fresh ginger root*
> *2 tablespoons peanut butter*
> *1 tablespoon soy sauce*
> *1 tablespoon sherry*
> *1½ tablespoons vinegar*
> *1 teaspoon sesame oil*
> *1 teaspoon Dijon mustard*
> *1 cup steamed carrots*
> *1 cup steamed broccoli*
> *3 scallions, finely chopped*

Boil the rotini until tender. Drain, saving ½ cup of the water.

Whir in a blender the ½ cup pasta water and the ginger, peanut butter, soy sauce, sherry, vinegar, sesame oil, and mustard. Toss pasta with sauce. Top with the carrots, broccoli, and chopped scallions.

★ SERVES 6

Gazpacho Salad

This summer salad is perfect for the peak of the tomato season, when the tomatoes are plentiful, ripe, and juicy. Interesting vinegar, such as sherry vinegar or a combination of balsamic and red wine vinegar, gives additional zest to this dish.

2 tablespoons olive oil
2 tablespoons sherry vinegar or 1 tablespoon balsamic and
*   1 tablespoon red wine vinegar*
Pinch of salt and freshly ground pepper
2 to 3 tablespoons fresh snipped basil
1⅓ cups cooked brown rice, cooled to room temperature
1 cup sliced mushrooms
2 medium to large tomatoes, cut in wedges
⅓ cup red pepper strips
¼ cup sliced green onions, including green tops
3 tablespoons parsley
Additional fresh herbs such as rosemary, lemon thyme,
*   tarragon, or dill*

Combine oil, vinegar, salt and pepper, and herbs in a large bowl, mix well, and add remaining ingredients. Serve on a bed of lettuce leaves, such as red or butter lettuce.

★ SERVES 4

Dips, Salads, and Side Dishes

Namasu

. . . .

These "pickled" vegetables are a good addition to a Far East picnic. Their sweet-sour flavor is enhanced by the fresh ginger. The recipe should be made a day ahead.

> 3 cups thinly sliced cucumber
> 2 cups thinly sliced carrots, sliced on the diagonal
> ½ cup thinly sliced sweet onions (Vidalia, Walla Walla, or the like)
> 1 teaspoon salt
> 2 tablespoons brown sugar
> ½ cup rice vinegar or white wine vinegar
> 2 to 3 teaspoons finely minced fresh ginger root

Sprinkle the vegetable slices with the salt and let them drain in a colander for at least ½ hour. Then pat them dry with a paper towel.

Combine sugar, vinegar, and ginger, heat until sugar has dissolved, and while hot, pour the mixture over the vegetables. Cover and refrigerate overnight.

★ SERVES 6

Tomatoes Stuffed with Zucchini and Corn

. . . .

These stuffed tomatoes can be prepared ahead of time and served at room temperature, or cooked in the oven while your burgers are on the grill. Big juicy tomatoes fresh from the farmers' market or your own garden make these a special treat.

4 large tomatoes
Salt and freshly ground black pepper
1 large sweet onion, peeled and chopped
2 garlic cloves, peeled and chopped
1 tablespoon olive oil
1 medium zucchini, diced
¼ cup diced jicama
1 cup fresh or frozen corn
1 teaspoon cumin seeds
½ teaspoon chili powder
¼ cup chopped cilantro
Guacamole or fresh salsa for garnish (optional)

Preheat oven to 350 degrees.

Cut off but reserve the tops of the tomatoes. Scoop out the pulp, mix with salt and pepper, and put in the bottom of a lightly greased baking dish that is big enough to hold all the tomatoes. Sprinkle the insides of the tomatoes with salt, turn upside down, and let drain.

Sauté the onion and garlic in the olive oil until transparent. Add zucchini, jicama, corn, cumin, and chili powder. Cook briefly, adding the cilantro last. Season to taste with salt and freshly ground black pepper and spoon into tomatoes. Stand them on the bed of tomato pulp, put their tops on, and bake for 15 to 20 minutes. Just before serving garnish with guacamole or fresh salsa or additional cilantro sprigs.

★ SERVES 4

Dips, Salads, and Side Dishes

Cold Stuffed Grape Leaves

. . . .

These grape leaves add a special touch to a picnic: They are a great finger food and travel well. When Kate and Ned Schumann were living on their boat in the Mediterranean, a Turkish friend taught them how to make these delicious morsels. Amazingly, this impressive recipe could be made in the tiny galley of a sailboat. Although the recipe is not hard, the mere stuffing of 40 to 50 grape leaves can be time-consuming, so it is a project that is fun to do with several other people.

40 to 50 grape leaves (a 1-pound jar)
¾ cup long-grain rice
2 or 3 tomatoes, peeled and finely chopped
½ cup finely chopped green onions
¾ cup currants
¼ cup toasted pine nuts (optional)
¼ cup finely chopped parsley
2½ tablespoons dried mint
¼ teaspoon each cinnamon and allspice
Salt and coarsely ground black pepper
2 tomatoes, sliced
4 cloves garlic, peeled
⅓ cup olive oil
½ cup water
1 teaspoon sugar
Juice of 1 large lemon

Place drained grape leaves in a large bowl and pour boiling water over them; let soak for half an hour (be sure water gets between the layers of leaves). Drain, then cover with cold water and drain again. If the leaves still seem briny, repeat the process once again.

In a bowl mix the rice, chopped tomatoes, green onions, currants, optional pine nuts, herbs, spices, and salt and pepper to taste.

Stuff the leaves with the mixture: On a leaf with the vein side up, put a good heaping tablespoon of the rice mixture near the stem edge. Fold the stem end over once and then tuck in the sides and roll up, giving a slight squeeze to each roll as you finish.

Line a large pan with either tomato slices or torn grape leaves. On top of these, pack the stuffed grape leaves tightly, slipping whole garlic cloves between the leaves. Mix the olive oil with ½ cup water, sugar, and lemon juice, and pour over the leaves. Put a plate on top of the leaves to keep them from unwinding.

Cover and simmer very gently for about 2 hours. You will probably need to add more water as the liquid becomes absorbed. Cool and serve at room temperature.

Note: If you have refrigerated these stuffed grape leaves, be sure to remove them from the refrigerator several hours before serving; that way the rice won't be crunchy.

★ MAKES 40 TO 50, SERVES 12

No-Cholesterol Basil Macaroni Salad

· · · · · · · · · · · · · · · · · · · ·

1 pound macaroni twists
1 medium onion, peeled and finely chopped
2 stalks celery, thinly sliced
½ sweet red pepper, chopped
1 cup No-Cholesterol Basil Mayonnaise (page 84)
Salt and freshly ground black pepper

Cook the macaroni according to package directions and drain thoroughly. Mix with rest of ingredients. Add salt and pepper to taste. Refrigerate until completely cooled.

★ SERVES 8

Bulgur with Fresh Dill and Tofu

. . . .

This salad is a big hit in the vegetarian cooking classes taught by Gail Naftalin of Silver Spring, Maryland. In fact, one student, who swore she could not eat tofu, took one taste of this and became a tofu-loving convert on the spot. Look for umeboshi plum paste in Asian food markets or natural foods stores.

One 10-ounce package firm Mori-Nu Silken Tofu
½ cup chopped fresh dill
½ cup chopped fresh parsley
1 teaspoon umeboshi plum paste (optional)
2 teaspoons light miso
2 teaspoons dark sesame oil
1 tablespoon lemon juice
1 cup grated carrot
¼ cup chopped scallions
½ cup diced jicama or water chestnuts
2 cups cooked bulgur

Mash the tofu, dill, parsley, plum paste, miso, sesame oil, and lemon juice. Add the grated carrot, scallions, jicama or water chestnuts, and bulgur. Mix well. Serve as a salad on a bed of lettuce or as a stuffing for pita bread.

★ SERVES 6

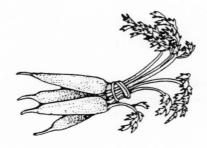

Gingery Baked Beans

• •

Your guests will love this spicier version of a picnic favorite. It was created by noted cookbook author and no-cholesterol cook, Mary McDougall.

2½ cups raw or 5 cups cooked navy beans
1 onion, peeled and chopped
One 16-ounce can tomatoes, chopped
2 tablespoons maple syrup
1 tablespoon apple cider vinegar
1 tablespoon soy sauce
1 tablespoon parsley flakes
1½ teaspoons dry mustard
1¼ teaspoons ground ginger
½ teaspoon cinnamon
¼ teaspoon black pepper

If raw beans are used, soak overnight and cook for 1½ hours or until tender.

Meanwhile, put chopped onion in saucepan with small amount of water and simmer for 10 minutes. Add remaining ingredients except for beans and stir for about 5 minutes. Then add beans and cook about 10 to 15 minutes to blend flavors.

★ SERVES 8

Nori Rolls

• • • • • • • • • • • • • • • • • • •

Nori is a sea vegetable used to make sushi. Nori rolls are a wonderful picnic item. They are indestructible, so they travel well. They can be eaten cold or at room temperature, they are packed with healthy ingredients, and they are fun to eat. Once you get the hang of making these, you'll find that it is fun to involve picnic guests in making their own.

You'll need to take a trip to a health food store or an Asian market to find some of these ingredients, such as nori, wasabi, rice syrup, ginger pickles, and umeboshi paste. You'll also need a sudare mat, found in the same stores. The recipe here is a very basic one, but you can create your own nori roll version with the addition of any favorite foods such as green beans, avocado, marinated tofu, ginger pickles, sesame seeds, shiitake mushrooms, jicama, or any leftover vegetables you have on hand.

¼ cup rice vinegar
¼ cup rice syrup
6 cups freshly cooked short- or medium-grain white or
*   brown rice*
10 nori sheets
½ teaspoon salt
1 peeled cucumber, seeded and sliced in long thin strips
10 green onions, sliced lengthwise into thin strips
2 carrots, sliced lengthwise into thin strips
½ cup ginger pickles

❦ **OPTIONAL SEASONINGS**
Umeboshi paste
Wasabi

❦ DIPPING SAUCE

½ cup low-sodium soy sauce or tamari

3 tablespoons water

2 tablespoons mirin (sweet rice wine) or sweet sherry

1 teaspoon grated or finely minced fresh ginger root

Mix together the vinegar and rice syrup. Pour over the rice while the rice is still warm.

Toast a nori sheet over a gas flame or an electric burner turned on high. As it gets done, it turns slightly lighter in color. Place the sheet of nori, shiny side down, on a sudare mat, about ½ inch away from the edge nearest you.

Spread about ½ cup of rice on the toasted nori, leaving a ½-inch border on the edge toward you and 2 inches uncovered at the far edge. Make a shallow trench crosswise along the center of the rice. Spread a line of umeboshi paste and some wasabi (not too much; wasabi is *very* hot) in the trench. Add 1 green onion and 1 or 2 thin slices *each* of cucumber, carrot and ginger pickle, being careful not to overfill. Begin to roll the sudare mat forward. The first roll should take you past the filling. Continue to roll, pressing firmly, but make sure the mat stays on top and doesn't get rolled inside. When you get to the far edge, moisten the nori with a little water and continue rolling to seal. When the roll is finished, slice it with a sharp knife into 6 equal pieces and arrange on a platter. Fill and roll the remaining nori sheets in the same way.

Mix the dipping sauce ingredients together and serve in a bowl with the nori.

★ SERVES 20

Dips, Salads, and Side Dishes

Salsa Verde

. . . .

Here is a spicy salsa to use as a dip or to dress up burgers. Look for tomatillos in the produce section of your grocery store. They look like little green tomatoes with a papery husk.

> *2 cups chopped tomatillos*
> *3 tablespoons chopped cilantro*
> *2 cloves garlic, peeled and roughly chopped*
> *1 small onion, peeled and cut into large chunks*
> *Juice of ½ lime*
> *Dash of sea salt*
> *Pinch of sugar*
> *½ teaspoon ground cumin*
> *½ teaspoon whole cumin seeds*
> *1 or 2 jalapeño or other medium hot peppers, seeded and*
>   *chopped*

Simmer the tomatillos in enough water to cover until not quite soft (about 6 minutes).

Combine all other ingredients and blend in processor until fairly smooth. Add drained tomatillos and blend until mixture is a chunky purée. Serve at room temperature as an accompaniment to bean burgers, tacos, or any Southwestern dish. This sauce also freezes well.

★ SERVES 12

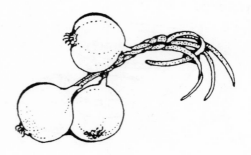

Zucchini Salad

• • • • • • • • • • • • • • • • • • • •

Deluged by prolific zucchini plants? Here's a refreshing salad that's quick and easy to prepare.

1¼ *pounds zucchini (about 3 medium)*
1½ *tablespoons olive oil*
2 *tablespoons tarragon vinegar*
2 *tablespoons each fresh snipped basil and mint (if fresh*
  herbs aren't available, use 2 teaspoons dried herbs)
1 *tablespoon fresh tarragon, or 1 teaspoon dried*
2 *tablespoons toasted pine nuts*

Shred the zucchini. Mix oil, vinegar, and herbs and pour over shredded zucchini. Toss in the pine nuts just before serving.

★ SERVES 4

No-Cholesterol Basil Potato Salad

• • • • • • • • • • • • • • • • • • • •

3 *pounds small, waxy new potatoes*
1 *medium onion, peeled and finely chopped*
2 *stalks celery, thinly sliced*
1 *cup No-Cholesterol Basil Mayonnaise (page 84)*
Salt and pepper to taste

Boil the whole potatoes in water until completely tender. Dice the potatoes. Add the onion, celery, and basil mayonnaise. Mix thoroughly. Add salt and pepper to taste.

★ SERVES 12

Black Beans Olé

. . . .

Black beans are a delicious staple of Mexican cooking. Give your picnic a south-of-the-border flavor with these spicy beans.

1½ cups uncooked black beans
1½ cups cooked corn
½ cup chopped sweet red pepper
¼ cup fresh lemon or lime juice
2 tablespoons canola oil
2 tablespoons tomato juice
½ teaspoon cumin seeds
1 package dried taco sauce mix
1 large bunch cilantro, chopped
1 bunch green onions, chopped, including some green tops

Cook beans in 5 cups water until tender. Combine beans, corn, and red pepper.

Mix together the lemon or lime juice, oil, tomato juice, cumin seeds, and taco sauce mix. Pour over the bean mixture.

Mix cilantro and green onions into the beans just before serving.

★ SERVES 8

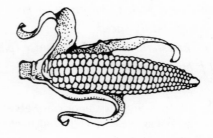

Watermelon Fire and Ice Salsa

Chopped watermelon gives this salsa a most unusual flavor and adds a touch of coolness to a spicy condiment.

> *3 cups chopped seeded watermelon*
> *½ cup chopped green peppers*
> *2 tablespoons lime juice*
> *1 tablespoon chopped cilantro*
> *1 tablespoon chopped green onions*
> *2 to 3 medium jalapeño peppers, seeded and chopped*
> *½ teaspoon garlic salt*
>
> *Fresh navel oranges, for garnish*
> *Watercress, for garnish*

Combine all ingredients except garnishes and mix well. Cover and refrigerate at least 1 hour. Serve on sliced oranges arranged on a bed of watercress.

★ SERVES 12

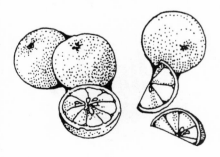

Dips, Salads, and Side Dishes

No-Cholesterol Basil Mayonnaise

· ·

You can still enjoy favorite picnic salads like potato and macaroni salads when you go cholesterol-free. This dressing, made from silken tofu, has no cholesterol and provides only half the fat of regular mayonnaise. And it offers one of the best flavors of summer—fresh basil—to make your salads extra special.

10½ ounces silken tofu
1 tablespoon white vinegar
1 tablespoon fresh lemon juice
½ teaspoon Dijon mustard
1 tablespoon olive oil
½ cup packed fresh basil leaves
Pinch of salt

Place all ingredients in a blender or food processor and blend until completely smooth. Keeps refrigerated for up to 2 weeks. Use as a sandwich spread or in salads.

★ MAKES 25 1-TABLESPOON SERVINGS

CHAPTER FIVE

Desserts

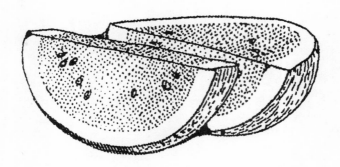

Top your picnics off with something sweet and special. We've offered some old-time favorites like cholesterol-free brownies and even have a couple of ideas for sweets to cook up on the grill.

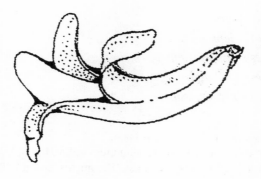

Gingered Melon Wedges

. . . .

Use cantaloupe or any other favorite melon for this recipe, which is a fast and elegant dessert.

> *1 large cantaloupe*
> *1 scant tablespoon powdered sugar*
> *½ teaspoon ground ginger*
> *1 tablespoon candied ginger (optional)*

Cut melon in half and seed. Then cut each half into chunks.

Stir together the sugar and ground ginger. Add candied ginger if you like. Sprinkle over melon chunks and chill.

★ SERVES 6

Grilled Apples with Cinnamon

. . . .

These are so much fun to make. This is a perfect dessert for early autumn cookouts when apples come into season.

> *4 large apples*
> *Juice of 1 lemon*
> *2 tablespoons margarine, melted*
> *1 tablespoon sugar*
> *¼ teaspoon cinnamon*

Slice apples and rub with lemon juice.

Place a piece of heavy-duty aluminum foil on the grill and brush it lightly with melted margarine. Place the apples on the foil in a single layer and cook over slow fire for 3 minutes. Flip the apple slices and cook for another 3 minutes. Brush lightly with melted margarine and sprinkle with sugar and cinnamon.

★ SERVES 4

Brownies

• •

These rich and chocolaty treats are always popular at picnics. Since they don't contain any eggs or animal fat, they are free of cholesterol and much lower in saturated fat than other chocolate desserts.

> 2 cups flour
> 2 cups sugar
> ½ cup cocoa
> 1 teaspoon baking powder
> ¼ teaspoon salt
> 1 cup water
> 1 cup vegetable oil
> 1 teaspoon vanilla
> ¼ cup chopped walnuts

Preheat oven to 350 degrees.

Sift the flour, sugar, cocoa, baking powder, and salt into a mixing bowl. Combine the water, oil, and vanilla and pour over the dry ingredients. Stir until well blended. Mix in the walnuts. Bake in a nonstick 9-× 13-inch pan for 25 to 30 minutes.

★ MAKES 24 BROWNIES

Here are two spectacular banana desserts. One can be made ahead for an easy, elegant presentation. The other is made right on the grill. Both taste indescribably rich for such low-fat dishes.

Grilled Bananas with Rum

. . . .

6 peeled bananas
2 tablespoons chopped candied ginger
2 tablespoons brown sugar
¼ cup dark rum
2 tablespoons orange juice
3 tablespoons margarine

Cut bananas in half lengthwise and place 2 halves in each of 6 large squares of aluminum foil. Add to each 1 teaspoon chopped ginger, 1 teaspoon brown sugar, 2 teaspoons rum, 1 teaspoon orange juice, and 1 teaspoon margarine. Fold over the edges of the foil and seal snugly.

Bake over hot coals for 5 or 6 minutes, until the bananas are soft and tender.

★ SERVES 6

Bananas Supreme

• •

This unusual dessert was given to Kate decades ago by a chef aboard a cruise ship. It has remained one of her favorites; it is wonderfully easy to make and although it tastes rich, it is low in fat. The only difficult thing about it is to remember to set aside 8 bananas to ripen (if you don't have ripe bananas don't make it—it doesn't have the same flavor).

½ cup golden raisins

5 tablespoons medium or dark rum, or *orange juice*

¼ cup packed light brown sugar

2 tablespoons softened margarine

8 very ripe bananas

2 tablespoons flour

1 tablespoon soy milk

In a small bowl press raisins in 2 tablespoons of the rum or orange juice. Let soak for 1 hour.

Preheat oven to 375 degrees. Cream together brown sugar and margarine until light and fluffy.

In another bowl mash bananas and then beat them into the sugar mixture with the remaining 3 tablespoons of dark rum or orange juice, the flour, and soy milk. Drain the raisins and stir into the banana mixture.

Pour the mixture into a 9-inch quiche pan that has been sprayed with Pam and bake until it is firm, about 45 minutes. (We use a pan that has a removable bottom and the "pie" slides out smoothly with a pretty fluted edge.) The dessert can be served either warm or at room temperature.

★ SERVES 8

Kiwi Sorbet

• • • • • • • • • • • • • • • • • • • •

An icy treat for the hottest summer days.

4 kiwi
One 6-ounce can lemonade concentrate, thawed
2 cups water

Peel the kiwi and process in blender or food processor just until smooth. (Do not crush the seeds.) Stir in lemonade concentrate and water. Pour mixture into a metal pan. Cover with foil and freeze until firm.

Remove from freezer and let stand 10 minutes. Break into small pieces and put into food processor. Process until smooth. Pack into a plastic container and cover. Return to freezer until firm. Serve by scooping.

★ SERVES 8

Fruit Popsicles

• • • • • • • • • • • • • • • • • • • •

A fun and easy-to-make treat for children.

1 ripe banana, peeled
1 ripe peach, peeled
6 to 8 strawberries, hulled
1 tablespoon brown sugar
¼ cup soy milk
¼ cup fruit juice (apricot nectar, orange juice, white grape
juice, or other juice of your choice)

Put all ingredients in a blender and process until smooth.

Pour into small paper cups and place on a tray in the freezer. Add popsicle sticks when the mixture has thickened slightly. Continue to freeze until firm.

★ SERVES 4

Orange Tofu Crème Brûlée

• • • • • • • • • • • • • • • • • • •

This is a sumptuous, cholesterol-free version of a favorite elegant dessert. It was created by Chef Peter Schaffroth of the Willard Hotel in Washington, D.C. To eliminate the cholesterol, this recipe uses a commercial egg replacer, which is a powdered egg-free product found in natural foods stores.

2 tablespoons egg replacer
¼ cup sugar, plus 2 tablespoons for caramelizing
1 cup Farm Rich–brand nondairy creamer
3 tablespoons soft tofu
Zest of 1 orange
1 tablespoon Grand Marnier

Preheat oven to 325 degrees.

Blend egg replacer and ¼ cup sugar together.

In a saucepan blend nondairy creamer, tofu, and orange zest, then heat and bring to a low boil. Add Grand Marnier. Pour the hot mixture over the sugar and egg replacer, stir well, and pour into four 3-ounce ramekins. Bake 20 minutes, set aside to cool, and sprinkle with remaining 2 tablespoons sugar.

Caramelize the sugar by placing under the broiler for less than a minute. It should be just slightly browned.

★ SERVES 4

Carrot Cake with Orange Glaze

. . . .

This is a super cake, chock-full of carrots, raisins, and other good things. Serve this at your next birthday party cookout.

1 cup chopped walnuts or other nuts
3½ cups whole wheat pastry flour
1 teaspoon sea salt
1 teaspoon cinnamon
1 tablespoon baking powder
½ cup canola oil
½ cup applesauce
½ cup apple juice
2 cups maple syrup
4 carrots, peeled and grated
2 tablespoons grated fresh ginger root
1 cup chopped golden raisins

Preheat oven to 350 degrees. Spread the nuts on a cookie sheet and bake 10 minutes or until light brown. Chop nuts and set aside.

Sift dry ingredients together. Combine the liquid ingredients and add them to the dry ones. Add the grated carrots, ginger, and raisins. Pour the batter into two 9-inch oiled layer cake pans and bake for 30 to 40 minutes, or until an knife inserted in the center comes out clean. Set aside to cool.

❦ GLAZE
Grated peel of 3 oranges
2 cups apple juice
Pinch of salt
2 tablespoons arrowroot powder dissolved in ½ cup water

Combine orange peel, apple juice, and salt in a saucepan and bring to a simmer. Combine arrowroot and water. Stir into the simmering liquid. Cook, stirring, until the mixture is thick. Set aside to cool.

Spread the glaze over 1 layer of cake. Place the second layer on top, spread the remaining glaze over it, and sprinkle it with the chopped nuts.

★ SERVES 8 TO 10

Marinated Fruit Kebabs

• • • • • • • • • • • • • • • • • • • •

While the coals are still hot from your burgers, try grilling some fresh marinated fruit for a refreshing, fat-free dessert.

6 ripe peaches, peeled and cut in quarters
3 bananas, peeled and thickly sliced
1 fresh pineapple, cubed
Chunks of cantaloupe or honeydew melon

❧ **MARINADE**
1 cup orange juice
¼ cup lime juice
½ cup brown sugar
1 tablespoon fresh chopped mint
2 tablespoons Cointreau, or any fruit-flavored liqueur

Mix the marinade ingredients and marinate the fruit for at least 30 minutes. Broil on skewers for about 5 minutes, basting often with the marinade.

★ SERVES 8

Desserts

Watermelon or Cantaloupe Sorbet

· · · · · · · · · · · · · · · · · · ·

If you have an ice cream maker, this sorbet is a snap to make. A scoop of it garnished with a wafer makes a lovely, elegant dessert for a summer lawn party.

❦ **SIMPLE SYRUP**
1 cup water
1 cup sugar

Heat water and sugar in small saucepan to boiling, stirring to dissolve sugar. Boil 5 minutes. Set aside to cool completely before using. Store in covered container in refrigerator for up to 1 month.

★ MAKES ABOUT 1½ CUPS

4 cups seeded 1-inch watermelon chunks, or 1-inch
    cantaloupe chunks (about 3 pounds cantaloupe)
½ cup Simple Syrup
2 tablespoons fresh lemon juice

Prepare the syrup.

Place melon in blender or food processor and blend until puréed. Add syrup and lemon juice. Whirl just to combine. Transfer to ice cream maker.

Freeze according to manufacturer's directions. Serve at once or transfer to freezer container. Freeze for up to 1 week. Soften in refrigerator for 30 minutes to 1 hour before scooping and serving.

★ SERVES 6

CHAPTER SIX

Beverages

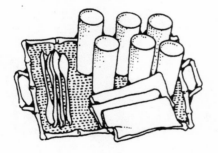

Hot summer days and sizzling barbecues need something icy and thirst-quenching. Beer and other alcoholic beverages dehydrate your body and raise your temperature, making you more thirsty and uncomfortable than before you had a drink. Very sweet beverages like sodas and fruit juices aren't always thirst-quenching, either. But fruit juices lightened with sparkling water or herbal teas and cooled down with fresh mint or citrus are lovely and refreshing on hot summer afternoons.

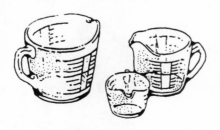

Kiwi Lime Cooler

• • • • • • • • • • • • • • • • • • •

Here is a summer refresher that is not too sweet.

8 ounces limeade
4 ripe kiwi, peeled
2 teaspoons sugar
8 ounces club soda

Place limeade, kiwi, and sugar in a blender and blend until kiwi is puréed. Mix with club soda and serve over ice.

★ SERVES 4

Tropical Dream

• • • • • • • • • • • • • • • • • • •

Sit back with a tall glass of this sweet, creamy tropical blend and you can just hear the breeze in the palm trees.

2 cups pineapple juice
1 cup orange juice
2 tablespoons cream of coconut

Pour all ingredients into a blender and blend until frothy. Serve over ice.

★ SERVES 4

Green Tea Cooler

• • • • • • • • • • • • • • • • • • • •

Green tea and ginger are very refreshing. Serve this as a punch when guests first arrive.

> *2-inch piece fresh ginger root, cut into quarters*
> *4 bags green tea*
> *1 tablespoon sugar*
> *4 cups boiling water*
> *32 ounces ginger ale*
> *Mint sprigs*

Place ginger, tea bags, and sugar in a pitcher. Pour boiling water over these and let steep at least ½ hour. Cool before adding ginger ale. Serve with ice and a sprig of mint.

★ SERVES 8

Minty Red Zinger Iced Tea

• • • • • • • • • • • • • • • • • • • •

Herbal tea laced with fresh mint is the best summer cooler imaginable.

> *2 to 3 Celestial Seasonings–brand Red Zinger tea bags*
> *½ to 1 cup fresh mint leaves*
> *1 tablespoon sugar*

Put all ingredients into a large teapot or pitcher and pour 6 cups boiling water over them. Let steep for at least 1 hour. Cool in refrigerator. Strain out the mint leaves and tea bags and serve over ice with a couple of fresh mint leaves for garnish.

★ SERVES 6

Peach-flavored Herbal Iced Tea

· ·

This herbal tea is sweet and spicy, perfect for after dinner.

3 herbal tea bags
2 cardamon pods
1 stick cinnamon
1 peach, peeled and sliced

Place all ingredients in a teapot or pitcher. Pour 6 cups boiling water over them. Let steep for at least 1 hour. Cool in refrigerator and remove tea bags. Serve over ice.

★ SERVES 6

Fruit Smoothie

· ·

Here is another frosty drink that is a hit with children.

1 banana, peeled, cut into chunks, and frozen
1 peach, peeled, cut into chunks, and frozen
6 strawberries, hulled
1 tablespoon brown sugar
⅓ cup soy milk
½ cup apple juice

Place all ingredients in a blender and blend until smooth.

★ SERVES 2

Minted Fruit Punch

• •

Mint comes in an astonishing variety of tastes and aromas, not just the familiar spearmint or peppermint. Most mints are attractive, easy-to-grow, sun-loving plants. Many are vigorous even to the point of being invasive. Try several of the following when you make this minted fruit punch: Ginger mint or emerald gold, Korean or anise mint, lemon mint, marigold mint or orange mint, sometime known as bergamot.

1 cup fresh mint leaves
1 cup water
1 cup sugar
1 sliced lime
6 ounces frozen orange juice concentrate
6 ounces frozen lemonade concentrate
48 ounces ginger ale

Wash and chop the mint. Boil water and sugar until sugar has dissolved. Pour over mint and lime. Add frozen juice. This makes a syrup concentrate that can be frozen for future use. Before serving, add ginger ale (or sparkling water if you prefer) to syrup and serve over ice. You can also add a cup of puréed fruit such as peaches, raspberries, or strawberries. Mix well and serve over ice.

★ SERVES 12

Beverages

Orange Sparkle

. . . .

Here is a wonderful blend of flavors that especially appeals to children.

5 cups orange juice, chilled
2 cups apricot nectar, chilled
1 cup grapefruit juice, chilled
2 cups cherry-flavored sparkling water, chilled
Ice cubes
Navel oranges, for garnish

Combine juices and sparkling water, stirring to blend. Cut oranges in half lengthwise. Place cut sides down; cut crosswise into thin half-cartwheel slices.

Serve juice over ice in tall glasses with a half-cartwheel orange slice in each for garnish.

★ SERVES 10

Picnic Menus for Special Occasions

• MEXICAN FIESTA •

Mexicali Burgers
Black Beans Olé
Tomatoes Stuffed with Zucchini and Corn
Salsa Verde
Jicama with Orange and Mint Salad
Cantaloupe Sorbet
Tropical Dream

• MIDDLE EASTERN GRILL •

Eggplant Dip
Vegetable Kebabs with Lemony Marinade
Cold Stuffed Grape Leaves
Bulgur with Fresh Dill and Tofu
Minty Red Zinger Iced Tea

• FAR EAST FEAST •

Grilled Five-Spice Tofu,
or *Grilled Tofu with Korean Barbecue Sauce*
Mystery Garden Oriental Salad
Namasu
Gingered Melon Wedges
Green Tea Cooler

• SUMMER LAWN PARTY WITH FINGER FOODS AND PUNCH •

Nasturtiums Filled with Guacamole
Raw vegetables with White Bean Dip with Lemon and Garlic
Cherry Tomatoes stuffed with Gazpacho Salad
Tempeh with Apricot Marinade
Kiwi Sorbet
Marinated Fruit Kebabs
Minted Fruit Punch

• CHILD'S BIRTHDAY PARTY •

P-Nutty Garden Burgers
Lentil Confetti Salad
Fruit Popsicles
Carrot Cake with Orange Glaze
Orange Sparkle

• OLD-FASHIONED FOURTH OF JULY FAMILY COOKOUT •

Garden Medley Vegetable Burgers
Mesquite-flavored Kebabs
Gingery Baked Beans
No-Cholesterol Basil Macaroni Salad
Peach-flavored Herbal Iced Tea
Brownies
Grilled Bananas with Rum

Recommended Cookbooks

• ESPECIALLY FOR BEGINNING VEGETARIAN COOKS •

American Wholefoods Cuisine
by Nikki and David Goldbeck
New American Library, 1983

*The Complete Whole Grain
Cookbook*
by Carol Gelles
Donald Fine, 1989

The New Laurel's Kitchen
by Laurel Robertson, Carol
Flinders, and Brian Ruppenthal
Ten Speed Press, 1986

Simply Vegan
by Debra Wasserman and Reed
Mangels
The Vegetarian Resource Group,
1991

· FOR ALL VEGETARIAN COOKS ·

The Complete Vegetarian Cuisine
by Rose Elliot
Fodors Travel, 1990

Cooking Under Pressure
by Lorna Sass
William Morrow and Company,
1987

Flowers in the Kitchen
by Susan Belsinger
Interweave Press, 1991

Moosewood Cookbook
by Mollie Katzen
Ten Speed Press, 1992

Recipes From an Ecological Kitchen
by Lorna Sass
William Morrow and Company,
1992

*Superb Vegetarian Cooking Under
Pressure*
by Lorna Sass
William Morrow and Company,
1994

The Vegetarian Epicure
by Anna Thomas
Vintage, 1972

*World of the East: Vegetarian
Cooking*
by Madhur Jaffrey
Alfred A. Knopf, 1982

Index

Index